$1.95

The Reproductive System

YOUR BODY How It Works

YOUR BODY
How It Works

The Reproductive System

Randolph W. Krohmer, Ph.D.

Introduction by
Denton A. Cooley, M.D.
President and Surgeon-in-Chief
of the Texas Heart Institute
Clinical Professor of Surgery at the
University of Texas Medical School, Houston, Texas

CHELSEA HOUSE
PUBLISHERS
A Haights Cross Communications Company ®
Philadelphia

CHELSEA HOUSE PUBLISHERS

VP, New Product Development Sally Cheney
Director of Production Kim Shinners
Creative Manager Takeshi Takahashi
Manufacturing Manager Diann Grasse

Staff for THE REPRODUCTIVE SYSTEM

Editor Beth Reger
Production Editor Megan Emery
Photo Editor Sarah Bloom
Series & Cover Designer Terry Mallon
Layout 21st Century Publishing and Communications, Inc.

www.chelseahouse.com

3 5 7 9 8 6 4 2

Library of Congress Cataloging-in-Publication Data

Krohmer, Randolph W.
   The reproductive system/Randolph W. Krohmer.
      p. cm.—(Your body, how it works)
Contents: Reproduction—Early embryonic development—Development
of the reproductive systems—Development differences in brain and
behavior—Puberty and beyond—Puberty in the male—Puberty in
the female—Concerns and complications.
   ISBN 0-7910-7629-6
   1. Reproduction—Juvenile literature. [1. Reproduction.] I. Title.
II. Series.
QP251.5.K76 2003
612.6—dc22
                                                     2003016807

Table of Contents

Introduction

The human body is an incredibly complex and amazing structure. At best, it is a source of strength, beauty, and wonder. We can compare the healthy body to a well-designed machine whose parts work smoothly together. We can also compare it to a symphony orchestra in which each instrument has a different part to play. When all of the musicians play together, they produce beautiful music.

From a purely physical standpoint, our bodies are made mainly of water. We are also made of many minerals, including calcium, phosphorous, potassium, sulfur, sodium, chlorine, magnesium, and iron. In order of size, the elements of the body are organized into cells, tissues, and organs. Related organs are combined into systems, including the musculoskeletal, cardiovascular, nervous, respiratory, gastrointestinal, endocrine, and reproductive systems.

Our cells and tissues are constantly wearing out and being replaced without our even knowing it. In fact, much of the time, we take the body for granted. When it is working properly, we tend to ignore it. Although the heart beats about 100,000 times per day and we breathe more than 10 million times per year, we do not normally think about these things. When something goes wrong, however, our bodies tell us through pain and other symptoms. In fact, pain is a very effective alarm system that lets us know the body needs attention. If the pain does not go away, we may need to see a doctor. Even without medical help, the body has an amazing ability to heal itself. If we cut ourselves, the blood clotting system works to seal the cut right away, and the immune defense system sends out special blood cells that are programmed to heal the area.

During the past 50 years, doctors have gained the ability to repair or replace almost every part of the body. In my own field of cardiovascular surgery, we are able to open the heart and repair its valves, arteries, chambers, and connections. In many cases, these repairs can be done through a tiny "keyhole" incision that speeds up patient recovery and leaves hardly any scar. If the entire heart is diseased, we can replace it altogether, either with a donor heart or with a mechanical device. In the future, the use of mechanical hearts will probably be common in patients who would otherwise die of heart disease.

Until the mid-twentieth century, infections and contagious diseases related to viruses and bacteria were the most common causes of death. Even a simple scratch could become infected and lead to death from "blood poisoning." After penicillin and other antibiotics became available in the 1930s and '40s, doctors were able to treat blood poisoning, tuberculosis, pneumonia, and many other bacterial diseases. Also, the introduction of modern vaccines allowed us to prevent childhood illnesses, smallpox, polio, flu, and other contagions that used to kill or cripple thousands.

Today, plagues such as the "Spanish flu" epidemic of 1918–19, which killed 20 to 40 million people worldwide, are unknown except in history books. Now that these diseases can be avoided, people are living long enough to have long-term (chronic) conditions such as cancer, heart failure, diabetes, and arthritis. Because chronic diseases tend to involve many organ systems or even the whole body, they cannot always be cured with surgery. These days, researchers are doing a lot of work at the cellular level, trying to find the underlying causes of chronic illnesses. Scientists recently finished mapping the human genome, which is a set of coded "instructions" programmed into our cells. Each cell contains 3 billion "letters" of this code. By showing how the body is made, the human genome will help researchers prevent and treat disease at its source, within the cells themselves.

The body's long-term health depends on many factors, called risk factors. Some risk factors, including our age, sex, and family history of certain diseases, are beyond our control. Other important risk factors include our lifestyle, behavior, and environment. Our modern lifestyle offers many advantages but is not always good for our bodies. In western Europe and the United States, we tend to be stressed, overweight, and out of shape. Many of us have unhealthy habits such as smoking cigarettes, abusing alcohol, or using drugs. Our air, water, and food often contain hazardous chemicals and industrial waste products. Fortunately, we can do something about most of these risk factors. At any age, the most important things we can do for our bodies are to eat right, exercise regularly, get enough sleep, and refuse to smoke, overuse alcohol, or use addictive drugs. We can also help clean up our environment. These simple steps will lower our chances of getting cancer, heart disease, or other serious disorders.

These days, thanks to the Internet and other forms of media coverage, people are more aware of health-related matters. The average person knows more about the human body than ever before. Patients want to understand their medical conditions and treatment options. They want to play a more active role, along with their doctors, in making medical decisions and in taking care of their own health.

I encourage you to learn as much as you can about your body and to treat your body well. These things may not seem too important to you now, while you are young, but the habits and behaviors that you practice today will affect your physical well-being for the rest of your life. The present book series, YOUR BODY: HOW IT WORKS, is an excellent introduction to human biology and anatomy. I hope that it will awaken within you a lifelong interest in these subjects.

Denton A. Cooley, M.D.
President and Surgeon-in-Chief
of the Texas Heart Institute
Clinical Professor of Surgery at the
University of Texas Medical School, Houston, Texas

1

Reproduction: A Characteristic of Life

The fact that this book is not a living organism should not be much of a surprise to anyone over the age of five. But how do we *know* that it is an **inanimate** object? The scientific community has developed a list of characteristics that can be used to determine if an object is truly alive. One of those characteristics is the ability to reproduce, ensuring the continued existence of the organism's population. Although this book was reproduced many times on a printing press, the book itself has no self-regulating mechanism to reproduce its own pages. However, all living organisms, from a single-celled amoeba to a 72 trillion-celled human have an **innate** drive to reproduce. It is a drive, not just a desire. Drive is something that must at least be tried if not accomplished.

There are two kinds of reproduction: asexual and sexual. Many biochemical events must occur before an organism can reproduce either way. Asexual reproduction is the simplest form of reproduction. Asexual literally means "without sex." In organisms that reproduce asexually, there are no males or females and reproduction occurs without partners coming together. Asexual, single-celled animals grow to a certain stage or size and will then divide into two identical organisms. This division is a complex process, requiring the organized division of genetic material, **mitosis** (Figure 1.1), to be coordinated with the division of the cytoplasm, **cytokinesis**, to form the **daughter cells**.

Multicelled asexual organisms have developed several unique reproductive strategies. For example, the jellyfish reproduces by budding, a process where a new individual begins to grow (bud) from the original organism and is eventually released as a small, free swimming organism. Starfish have a similar method of reproduction. More than 100 years ago, men working the oyster beds wanted to eradicate starfish because the starfish would eat the oysters before they were large enough to take to market. When workers brought up a starfish with their catch, they would cut it into pieces and throw it back into the water thinking they had put an end to that starfish. Little did the workers know, the starfish has a unique mode of reproduction through which an entire starfish can be regenerated from each piece. Obviously, this put the oyster farmers at an even greater disadvantage as they caused an increase in the population rather than wiping it out. Asexual plants, such as strawberries, propagate new individuals by sending out shoots that will develop into new plants. This is also how new plants can be generated from "cuttings" of existing plants. All of these reproductive methods produce offspring that are **clones** (genetically identical) to the organism from which they originated.

The benefits of asexual reproduction include the fact that all organisms can reproduce. That is, no individual is dependent on another to reproduce. Organisms that reproduce by asexual means are capable of creating a large population in a relatively short time. Because the organisms are genetically identical, they will all be equally successful in the same constant environment. The genetic similarities, however, confer some disadvantages to asexual organisms. For example, if a population of clones is perfectly suited for an environment that has a pH of 7.0 and a temperature range between 25–30° C, what happens if the environment changes? If the temperature increases and the pH of the environment becomes more acidic, the population has no genetic variability and, therefore, no way to compensate for changes in their surroundings. What most

(continued on page 14)

11

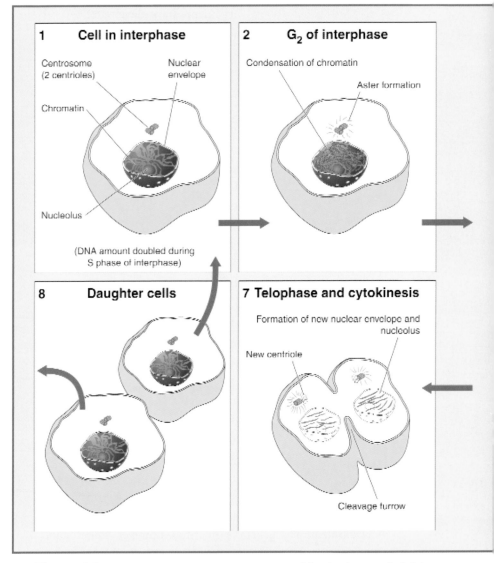

Figure 1.1 Mitosis is the organized process resulting in the equal division of the nucleus. When combined with cytokinesis (division of the cytoplasm), the process forms two identical cells or clones. During **interphase**, the cell grows and the genetic material contained within the nucleus is duplicated. Following this period of preparation, the cell enters **prophase** in which the nuclear envelope breaks down, and the paired asters (centrioles) migrate to opposite sides of the cell while sending out fibers, forming the mitotic spindle. During **metaphase**, the chromosomes line up in the middle of the cell and fibers from both centrioles

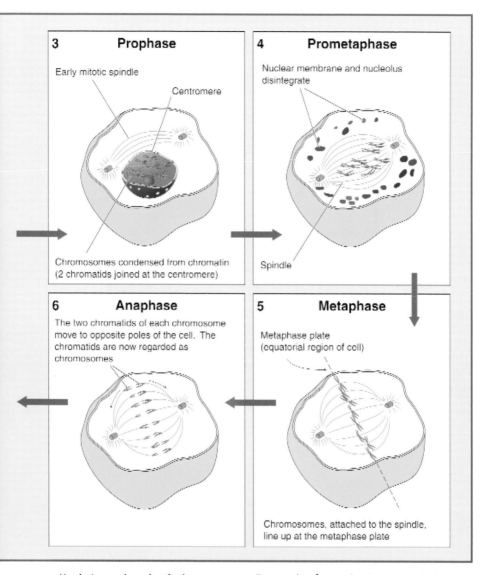

3   Prophase

Early mitotic spindle

Centromere

Chromosomes condensed from chromatin
(2 chromatids joined at the centromere)

4   Prometaphase

Nuclear membrane and nucleolus
disintegrate

Spindle

6   Anaphase

The two chromatids of each chromosome
move to opposite poles of the cell. The
chromatids are now regarded as
chromosomes

5   Metaphase

Metaphase plate
(equatorial region of cell)

Chromosomes, attached to the spindle,
line up at the metaphase plate

attach to each pair of chromosomes. **Prometaphase** is the stage during
which the nuclear membrane begins to disintegrate. During **anaphase**, the
daughter chromosomes are pulled by the spindle fibers to opposite sides of the
cell and by late anaphase, as the daughter chromosomes near their destination, a
cleavage furrow begins to form in the cell membrane indicating the beginning
of **cytokinesis**. In the final stage, **telophase**, the cell membrane continues to
constrict and eventually divides into daughter cells. As this is occurring, the
nucleus is reestablished, and the daughter cells are once again in prophase.

(continued from page 11)

likely will happen under these circumstances is that the entire population will disappear because it could not tolerate or live in the new environment.

Sexual reproduction is much more complex, but offers the benefit of genetic variability. This method of reproduction may waste some nutrients on males who cannot add to the population number directly, but they offer a different set of chromosomes that generates genetic variability, allowing sexually reproducing species to evolve and occupy essentially every corner of the earth. Unlike mitosis which copies the exact genetic blueprint before each cell division, sexual reproduction must take into account that when combining two cells during fertilization, the resulting cell cannot exceed the genetic material present in the **somatic** (non-sex) cells of that species. In humans, all of the cells in the body are considered somatic cells except for the egg and sperm that are categorized as sex cells. Somatic cells contain all of the genetic information that makes you who and what you are. This genetic information is contained on 23 pairs (46 total) of chromosomes housed within the nucleus. Chromosomes are the blueprint that makes each individual unique. They are composed of millions upon millions of DNA molecules that in turn code for (or direct) the development of each and every characteristic of an individual such as hair, skin, and eye color. In somatic cells, each pair of chromosomes represents equally the genetic information from each of the parents. Sex cells develop by **meiosis** (Figure 1.2), a process that requires the **stem cell** to go through two nuclear divisions during which the genetic material is reshuffled and reduced by half, forming the **eggs** or **sperm**.

Because the meiotic process is very efficient at mixing up the genetic material, and each individual has an equal complement from both mother and father, no two individuals (except for identical twins) have exactly the same genetic profile. Although you and your **siblings** (brothers and/or sisters) may have characteristics in common, such as the color of hair and eyes, hundreds and maybe even thousands of other characteristics within your **genetic profile** make you a unique individual. Because each individual is so unique, each person can now be identified by his or her specific genetic profile. This profile is most commonly used in law enforcement to convict and sometimes exonerate suspects in a crime.

CONGRATULATIONS, IT'S A GIRL . . . AND A BOY!

Although born in the same hour of the same day and year, Sarah is considered to be Andrew's big sister because she was born a full eight minutes before he emerged. Obviously not identical, because one is female and the other male, Sarah and Andrew are **fraternal** twins (Figure 1.3).

Andrew and Sarah's story actually begins long before birth. In fact, the developmental process, called pregnancy, began approximately nine months earlier. The human **ovary** usually releases (**ovulates**) a single egg (**ovum**) during a female's monthly menstrual cycle. However, their mother's ovaries released two **ova** instead of the normal one (Figure 1.4).

In what can only be viewed as the competition to end all competitions, several hundred million **spermatozoa** move through the uterus and into the **fallopian tubes** in search of an ovum to fertilize.

The ova that have just been released begin their journey down the fallopian tube to the uterus where, if fertilized, they will develop and grow during the next nine months. The competition ultimately ends when the strongest, and indeed luckiest (as there is a certain aspect of luck involved) **sperm** locates and successfully fertilizes an ovum. In the present competition, two sperm are declared winners as each was able to fertilize one of the eggs that will eventually develop into the twins, Sarah and Andrew.

Why are the twins a boy and a girl? Could they have been two boys or two girls? In actuality, the chances were just as good for our twins to be the same sex.

(continued on page 18)

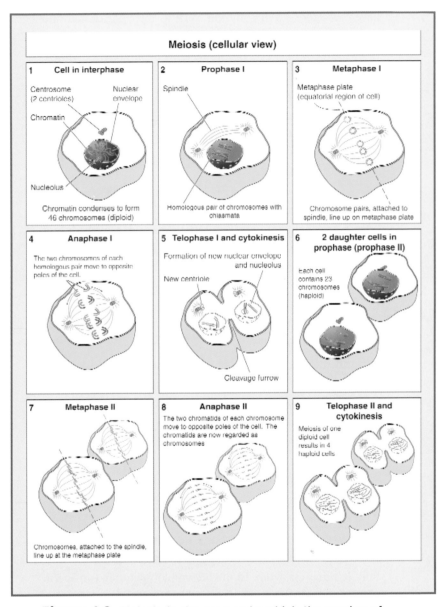

Figure 1.2 Meiosis is the process by which the number of chromosomes in gametes (egg or sperm) are reduced by half (haploid). During meiosis I, chromosome pairs are drawn to opposite poles of the cell, establishing genetic variation. Following telophase I, the cell enters a resting stage called interkinesis

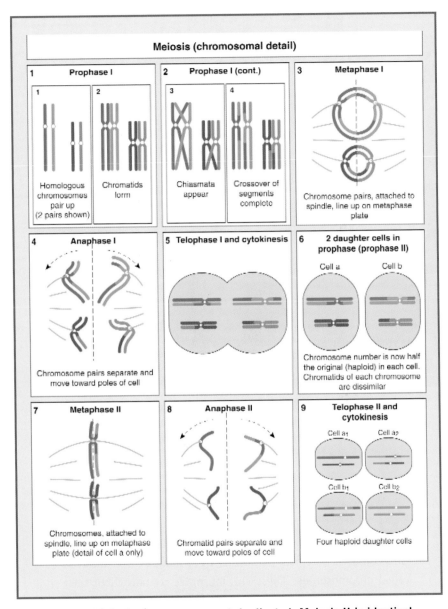

Meiosis (chromosomal detail)

1   Prophase I

1   2

Homologous chromosomes pair up (2 pairs shown)   Chromatids form

2   Prophase I (cont.)

3   4

Chiasmata appear   Crossover of segments complete

3   Metaphase I

Chromosome pairs, attached to spindle, line up on metaphase plate

4   Anaphase I

Chromosome pairs separate and move toward poles of cell

5   Telophase I and cytokinesis

6   2 daughter cells in prophase (prophase II)

Cell a   Cell b

Chromosome number is now half the original (haploid) in each cell. Chromatids of each chromosome are dissimilar

7   Metaphase II

Chromosomes, attached to spindle, line up on metaphase plate (detail of cell a only)

8   Anaphase II

Chromatid pairs separate and move toward poles of cell

9   Telophase II and cytokinesis

Cell a₁   Cell a₂

Cell b₁   Cell b₂

Four haploid daughter cells

in which chromosomes are not duplicated. Meiosis II is identical to mitosis with the individual chromosomes moving to opposite poles. However, without chromosome duplication, each daughter cell receives only half of the normal complement of chromosomes.

Figure 1.3 Sarah (left) and Andrew are the twins who will serve as our example for the reproductive process. Although they look quite similar, they are not identical, as two separate eggs were fertilized during the reproductive process.

(continued from page 15)

What actually determines the sex of an individual? To answer that question, it is important to determine why and how males and females differ from each other. All living organisms contain a blueprint made of **DNA** contained on structures called **chromosomes**. These chromosomes contain all of the information that makes each person who he or she is. In humans, this collection of genetic material is carried on 46 chromosomes (**diploid**), half of which came from the mother and half from the father (**haploid**).

Recall that chromosomes composed of millions of DNA

molecules were said to be the blueprint from which each individual develops. Forty-four of the 46 chromosomes in the human somatic cells are called **autosomal** chromosomes and carry the information for all of the characteristics that make up an individual, except for sexual determination. The remaining two chromosomes, one donated by each parent, are **sex chromosomes** (designated as either X or Y). Their function is to assign (or determine) the sex of an individual. If the combination of sex chromosomes is XX, the individual will be female. If XY, the individual will be male.

During the production and development of both sperm and ova, the number of chromosomes is divided in half by the process of meiosis. So, when an ovum containing 23 chromosomes is fertilized by a sperm containing 23 chromosomes, the total number of chromosomes in the embryo is restored to 46. If the number of chromosomes is reduced by 50% during meiosis, the sex chromosomes will also be reduced by 50%, so that only one sex chromosome can be carried by each sperm or egg. If you separate the sex chromosomes in a female (XX), you will find that the only type of sex chromosome that can be donated to an egg is an X (female). On the other hand when you separate the sex chromosomes in a male (XY), half of the sperm contain an X chromosome (female) and the other half contain a Y chromosome (male). It should now be obvious that it is the sperm (male gamete) that determines the sex of an individual.

What occurred during fertilization that produced our

TESTING THIS ASSUMPTION

Take two coins; let heads represent females and tails represent males. Flip the two coins simultaneously 30 times, recording the outcome of each trial. Chances are you will be relatively close to equal numbers of tails:heads (boy:girl), tails:tails (boy:boy), and heads:heads (girl:girl).

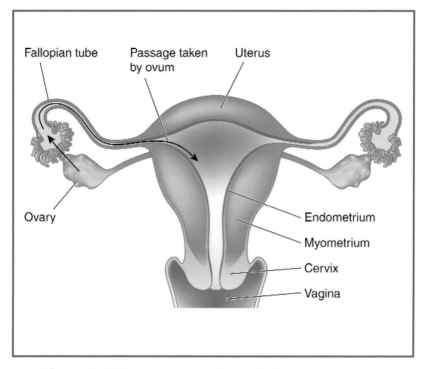

Fallopian tube

Passage taken by ovum

Uterus

Ovary

Endometrium

Myometrium

Cervix

Vagina

Figure 1.4 This cross section of the fallopian tubes and uterus demonstrates the pathway an ovum (egg) must take to reach the uterus. At ovulation, the upper end of the fallopian tube becomes active, sweeping over the surface of the ovary. As the egg is ejected from the ovary it is swept into the fallopian tube and begins the journey to the uterus.

fraternal twins was a random, chance event, resulting in two children, one female and one male. The essential feature of sexual reproduction is that the new individual receives its genetic endowment in two equal portions, half carried by the sperm and half carried by the ovum. Because Sarah's and Andrew's parents contributed roughly equal portions of the twins' DNA blueprint, they have many of the same chromosomes that determine many of the same characteristics. This is why both of our twins have blond hair, green eyes, and freckles. In terms of their reproductive systems, however, Sarah and Andrew are very different.

By studying Sarah and Andrew from embryonic development to puberty and then adulthood, we can examine the
differences in human reproductive systems.

CONNECTIONS

Conception is dependent on a sperm locating and fertilizing an
egg. Once fertilized, the egg, now combined with the genetic
material from the sperm to form a structure referred to as a
zygote, begins a process resulting in the birth of an individual.
The sex of that individual will depend solely on random
chance that the sperm fertilizing the egg will be carrying an X
sex chromosome (female) or a Y sex chromosome (male). The
chance that a child will be either female or male is 50:50. The
chances that our twins would be a girl and a boy were no better than having twins of the same sex.

CHROMOSOMAL MISTAKES

Occasionally, a chromosome pair does not separate during meiosis,
resulting in an inappropriate number of chromosomes in an egg or
sperm. Another relatively rare alteration in chromosomal organization occurs when a piece breaks off of a chromosome and is lost or
reattaches to another chromosome where it does not belong.

Most of these chromosomal alterations are never seen
because so many of the genes carried on the chromosomes are
critical for embryonic development. Any egg, sperm, or developing embryo with an error of an extra or missing chromosome
is unlikely to survive. However, a few alterations of autosomal
and sex chromosome number do result in live births. The most
common autosomal alteration, Down's syndrome, also known as
trisomy 21, is the result of having three copies of chromosome 21.
Less common are Edwards' syndrome (trisomy 18) and Patau's
syndrome (trisomy 13). The four most common alterations in
the number of sex chromosomes include double-Y syndrome
(XYY), Klinefelter's syndrome (XXY), trisomy-X syndrome (XXX),
and Turner's syndrome (XO).

2

Early Embryonic Development

As you have already discovered, fertilization occurs when the sperm with its complement of genetic information enters the egg and combines with the chromosomes contained in the egg, forming a new genetic blueprint and initiating the formation of a zygote. In the case of Sarah and Andrew, the sperm successfully fertilizing the ovum that will eventually develop into Sarah carried an X sex chromosome. The sperm fertilizing the ovum that developed into Andrew carried a Y sex chromosome (Figure 2.1).

Early development of the tissues that will eventually be transformed into the testes or ovaries is identical in both the male and female. In this early stage, the future **gonads** are made up of the same two tissues, **somatic** tissue that will form the bulk of the gonadal matrix, and **primordial germ cells** (**PGC**) that will, at a later time, **migrate** into this tissue mass and transform into **gametes** (sperm or ova). In human embryos, the future gonads develop between 3.5–4.5 weeks after conception. A short time later, columns of cells formed by inward migration and cellular division invade the center of the future gonad and form the primary internal structures called **primitive sex cords**.

At about three weeks after conception, the primordial germ cell population increases dramatically by mitosis and begins to migrate towards the future gonad. Approximately 30 days after conception, the majority of the PGCs have migrated into the area of the future gonad. There, they form small clusters or colonies of cells that take

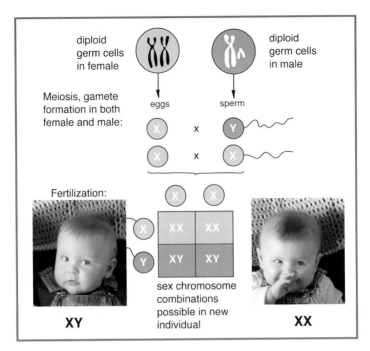

Figure 2.1 This figure depicts the genetics of sex determination in a developing embryo. Because the sperm can carry an X (female) or a Y (male) sex chromosome (the egg can supply an X sex chromosome only), it is the sex-determining factor of an individual.

up residence within and between the developing primitive sex cords. During this period of PGC migration and early colonization, it is not possible to distinguish between the male and female gonads, which are referred to as "**indifferent.**"

In male embryos, the Y chromosome becomes active in determining gonadal sex only after migration and colonization of the PGCs has been completed, approximately six weeks after fertilization. Tissues that make up the outer cortex of the gonad condense and form a tough fibrous cover called the **tunica albuginea.** In the center of the tissue matrix, the sex cords grow and develop into the testis cords that will incorporate most of the PGCs (that have now completed mitosis) and separate from the surrounding tissue by forming an outer layer called the **basement membrane**. These structures are then known as the seminiferous cords that eventually give rise to the **seminiferous tubules** of the adult. Of the two cell populations within the seminiferous cords, the PGCs will develop into the **spermatogonia** (stem cells) that will be responsible for the continued sperm production throughout a male's adult life. The remaining cells of the seminiferous cords give rise to the **Sertoli cells** that make up the internal **epithelial layer** of the future seminiferous tubules. Blood vessels can be seen invading the loose tissue between the cords while the cells appear to condense, forming the endocrine units of the testes, called the **interstitial cells of Leydig**.

While the male gonad is undergoing all of these changes, the female gonad has remained in an indifferent phase. In fact, at this developmental stage, the only way to recognize a gonad as a potential ovary is by its failure to develop seminiferous cords and by its continued division of PGCs within the matrix of the

DID YOU KNOW?

It has only been within the past 125 years that the sperm's role in fertilization has been known. The Dutch microscopist, Anton van Leeuwenhoek, codiscovered sperm in 1678, at which time he believed sperm to be parasitic animals living within the semen, coining the name spermatozoa meaning "sperm animals." Originally, he assumed sperm had nothing to do with reproducing the organism in which they were found. Later, van Leeuwenhoek was under the belief that each sperm contained a preformed embryo. In 1685, van Leeuwenhoek wrote, "sperm are seeds (both sperm and semen mean "seed") and that the female only provides the nutrient soil in which the seeds are planted." However, van Leeuwenhoek tried for many years and never found preformed embryos within the spermatozoa. Nicolas Hartsoeker, the other codiscoverer of sperm, drew a picture of what he hoped to find: a preformed human (homunculus) within each human sperm. Today, there is no question about the role of sperm in the reproductive process.

future gonad. The primitive sex cords of the female remain disorganized and will eventually disappear as blood vessels invade the interior, creating a highly vascular center in the female gonad. At about 16 weeks, the tissues that make up the outer layers of the primitive ovary begin to break up into isolated cell clusters forming the **primordial follicles**. Each follicle consists of an **oogonium** derived from a PGC that is surrounded by a single layer of flattened follicular cells derived from the tissues of the outer cortex. Active mitosis of **oogonia** (stem cells for egg development) continues, developing as many as 5 million primordial follicles during a female's fetal life. Immediately before birth, active mitosis ends, and no more oogonia are produced during the remainder of the female's life.

The migration and presence of PGCs into the genital ridge does not have any role in determining the sex of an individual nor does it initiate gonadal **differentiation**. The visible changes that can be seen between the gonads of male and female embryos depend only on the presence or absence of the Y chromosome that has taken charge of male development. The presence of a Y chromosome transforms an indifferent gonad into a testis. The absence of the Y chromosome results in the indifferent gonad developing into an ovary.

The primary role of the sex chromosomes, specifically the Y chromosome, in determining the sex of an embryo is completed when the sex of the fetal gonad has been established. From this point on, genetic sex is relatively unimportant. Instead, the gonads assume the active role in directing the rest of sexual development, both during the remainder of embryonic development as well as after birth (Figures 2.2 and 2.3).

In the male embryo, the testis takes over sexual development through the synthesis and release of hormones needed for the complete and accurate development of the male embryo. The interstitial cells of Leydig synthesize and secrete the male hormones called **androgens**. Androgens comprise a group of **steroid** hormones that include **testosterone** (the "male

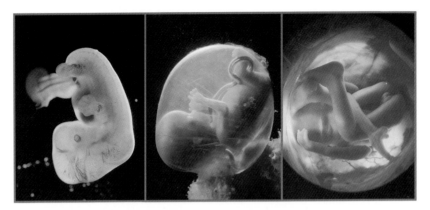

Figure 2.2 These photographs (L to R) depict a human embryo at 5, 14, and 20 weeks post-conception. At 5 weeks, the embryo has initiated the development of both the upper and lower limbs and has pigmented eyes situated on either side of the developing head. By week 14, the lower limbs are fully formed and you can see the early development of toenails. The eyes now face forward and the ears are close to their normal position. By week 20, arms and fingers are fully formed, head and body hair are now visible and quickening (signs of life) can be felt by the mother. Week 20 is considered the last developmental stage of previable fetuses.

hormone") and **dihydrotestosterone**. Another important hormone during early development of the male embryo is **Müllerian inhibiting factor (MIF)**. This hormone is produced by the Sertoli cells within the seminiferous cords of the developing testes (see Chapter 3). The presence of androgens and MIF directs male sexual differentiation throughout the body.

In contrast, the release and/or presence of specific hormones, also referred to as endocrine activity, is not required for the sexual differentiation of the ovaries during fetal life. Therefore, in the absence of androgens, development will proceed as female. It is extremely important to note that the developmental pathway leading to the development of a male embryo must be altered by genetic and hormonal influences to develop as a male. However, development of a female embryo requires no change in the developmental pathway that is already in place.

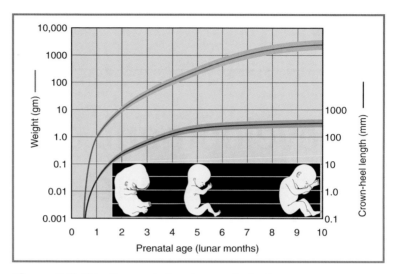

Figure 2.3 This diagram depicts the growth of a fetus, represented in weight gain and increase in length during the prenatal period. During the early stages of development, the fetus's limbs are just beginning to take shape. By the time of birth (9 months), the child is fully formed.

CONNECTIONS

Early in development, the reproductive systems of both males and females are identical and are said to be in an indifferent phase, meaning that there is no indication of the genetic sex of the embryo. The presence and eventual expression of the Y sex chromosome initiates the development of the testes in males. In the absence of the Y sex chromosome, the gonadal tissue will begin later to develop as an ovary. Once the testes have been determined and the interstitial cells of Leydig (endocrine cells of the testes) have initiated the synthesis and secretion of androgens, the role of genetic sex (influence of the sex chromosomes) is no longer needed. Essentially, the sex chromosomes no longer have a role in directing sexual development. From this point on, the testes will control male development. Females are essentially the default sex, developing in the absence of the Y sex chromosome or androgens. Without these influences the embryo will develop into a female.

3

Development of the Reproductive System

Once the fetal gonad has been determined by the presence or absence of the Y chromosome, the role of the sex chromosomes in dictating the genetic sex is rendered unimportant. Instead, the gonads now assume a leading role in all further development of the reproductive system through synthesis and release of chemical messengers called hormones. In this chapter, we will examine the development of the male and female reproductive systems (Figures 3.1 and 3.2) and the role of gonadal hormones in directing this development.

In both male and female embryos, the tissues that will form the structures of the internal **genitalia** are composed of two separate sets of embryonic tissues that are **unipotential**. That is, these tissues are destined to develop in only one way, either as structures in the female reproductive system or structures in the male reproductive system, but not both. These primordial structures, the **Wolffian ducts** and **Müllerian ducts**, are present in the early stages of both male and female embryonic development. In the female embryo, the absence of androgens results in the complete regression of the Wolffian ducts and allows the development of the Müllerian ducts. These ducts give rise to the female reproductive structures, oviducts, uterus, and cervix. If the gonads of the male are removed, the result is an absence of androgens in embryos of either sex, and the internal genitalia automatically develop according to the female pattern. This observation demonstrates that ovarian activity is not required for the development of the female reproductive tract.

In a normal developing male, the presence of hormones produced by the testes prevents the natural trend toward the development of female internal genitalia. Therefore, androgens, specifically testosterone and dihydrotestosterone, secreted in very large amounts by the interstitial cells of Leydig, induce the Wolffian ducts to develop and give rise to male structures, the **epididymis**, **vas deferens**, and **seminal vesicles**. These structures will compose a portion of the pathway in the adult male that allows sperm and associated secretions to exit the body. If androgens are not present during this stage of development, the Wolffian ducts will degenerate as they would in the female embryo.

Although androgens are crucial in the male embryo for the conversion of the Wolffian duct system into structures of the adult system, they have no influence on the development or regression of the Müllerian duct system. Unlike the Wolffian ducts that form an integral component of the male reproductive system, the Müllerian ducts are not utilized in males. These ducts should undergo a complete regression during embryonic development. However, regression of the Müllerian ducts will occur only if another testicular hormone, Müllerian inhibiting factor (MIF), is synthesized and secreted by the Sertoli cells contained within the developing seminiferous cords. Therefore, in the absence of MIF, the Müllerian duct system will develop as if it were located in a female embryo.

The tissues that will make up the external genitalia of males and females, unlike the internal genitalia, are **bipotential**, meaning they have the ability to develop in one of two ways depending on the presence or absence of the male gonad/hormone. In a female embryo, the **urethral folds** and **genital swellings** remain separate, forming the **labia minora** and **labia majora**. The **genital tubercle** will form the **clitoris**.

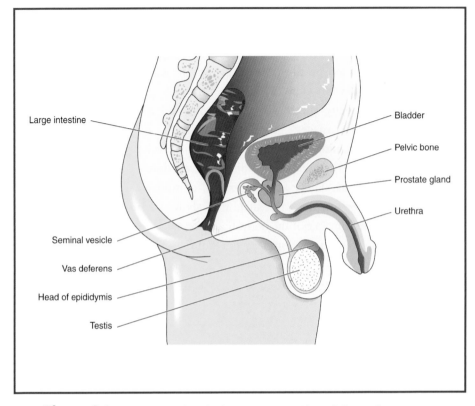

Large intestine

Bladder

Pelvic bone

Prostate gland

Urethra

Seminal vesicle

Vas deferens

Head of epididymis

Testis

Figure 3.1 This illustration depicts a cross section of the male reproductive system. Notice that the urethra is important to both urination and the release of sperm. Sperm produced in seminiferous tubules of the testes combine with secretions from the seminal vesicle, prostate gland, and bulbourethral glands (not labeled) to form a mixture called **semen**.

As with the internal genitalia of females, removal of the ovary will not alter this line of development, indicating that it is independent of any ovarian endocrine activity. Again, it is the secretion of androgens from the testes, specifically dihydrotestosterone, which causes the urethral folds to fuse along the midline. This action encloses the urethral tube and, with a portion of the genital swelling, forms the shaft of the penis. The remaining portion of the genital swelling fuses

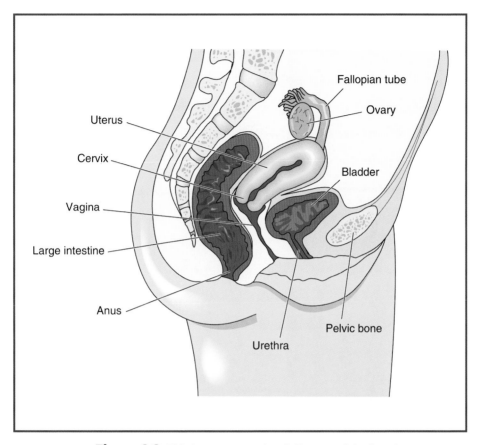

Figure 3.2 This is a cross-sectional diagram of the female reproductive system, showing the relationship of reproductive organs. In the female, the urethra does not have a dual purpose as in the male and is used for urination only. The ovaries are suspended from the abdominal wall above it and to each side of the uterus, and utilize the fallopian tubes (oviducts) to deliver the ovulated egg to the uterus. Each month, the uterus prepares for a possible pregnancy by increasing the endometrial lining and blood supply. Menstrual flow and a child are delivered through the cervix and vagina, also referred to as the birth canal.

at the midline forming the scrotum. The genital tubercle enlarges to form the **glans penis**. Androgen is critical for the development of the male external genitalia. Removal of the

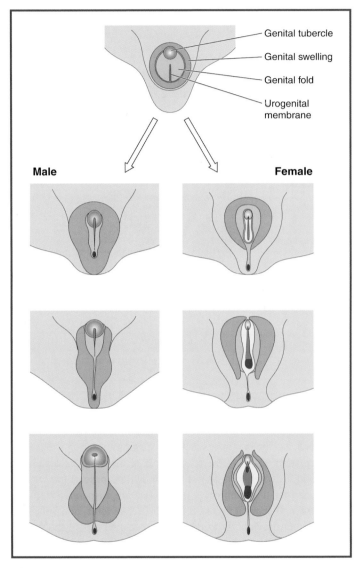

Figure 3.3 This diagram demonstrates the different developmental processes leading to male and female external genitalia. In the presence of the androgen dihydrotestosterone (DHT), the primordial genital structures will fuse to form the penis, which encloses the urethra and the scrotum. In the absence of any hormonal influence, the primordial genital structures will not fuse, and, thus, form the female genitalia instead.

testes, stopping androgen release, will result in the feminization of the external genitalia. Exposure of a female fetus to androgens will masculinize her external genitalia.

By weeks 16–20 of development, the testis consists of an outer fibrous tunica albuginea. This outer layer surrounds

TESTICULAR FEMINIZATION MUTATION (TFM)

The concept that all embryos will inherently develop along the female pathway can be demonstrated in genetic XY males who suffer from testicular feminization mutation (TFM). Some XY individuals have reproductive tissues that do not respond to the presence of androgens. This androgen insensitivity is due to the absence of functioning androgen receptors (structures that recognize androgens) in tissues that require androgens for the development along the male pathway. Because the Y chromosome is present, testicular development occurs along with elevated levels of prenatal and **postnatal** androgens. The testes also produce Müllerian inhibiting factor (MIF), which causes the regression of the Müllerian duct system. However, in these individuals, the Wolffian duct system does not recognize androgen and, therefore, does not develop. Males born with TFM have perfectly normal-appearing external female genitalia and are generally reared as girls. The parents and doctors are often unaware that the child is actually genetically male. This condition is usually discovered during adolescence when menstruation fails to occur. Because the Müllerian ducts fail to develop, the vagina is reduced in length and no uterus or fallopian tubes will develop. These individuals are sterile. In these individuals, estrogen receptors function normally. At puberty, the estrogen generated from excess androgens initiate the development of the secondary sex characteristics in a female direction.

highly vascular tissues that contain condensed Leydig cells and solid seminiferous cords. The cords contain Sertoli cells and the future germ cells, spermatogonia. The seminiferous cords develop into the seminiferous tubules where sperm are produced, requiring the development of a pathway for the release of the sperm. As the seminiferous cords develop, they contact and join the cords of the developing **rete testis**, which, in turn, lead directly to the **vasa efferentia**, the epididymis, and the vas deferens. The Leydig cells within the developing testis begin to secrete androgens as early as the eighth week of fetal life. They will continue to secrete hormones, in drastically varying amounts, throughout the life of the individual. During development of the male embryo, the level of circulating androgens reaches its highest concentration around 13–15 weeks, after which the circulating levels decline slowly, reaching a basal (baseline) level around 5–6 months into development. The presence of androgens is essential for establishing the internal and external of normal male reproductive **morphology**.

CONNECTIONS

Once the development of the testes is initiated and hormones are being synthesized and released into the circulation, genetic sex, imposed by the sex chromosomes, is no longer important. Hormones, specifically testosterone and dihydrotestosterone, play a critical role in developing the remaining male reproductive structures. Under the influence of testosterone, the Wolffian ducts will develop and form a portion of the sperm's pathway to the exterior. Dihydrotestosterone is necessary for the development of male external genitalia. MIF is responsible for the regression of the Müllerian duct system. In the absence of testosterone, dihydrotestosterone, and even estrogen from the female's ovary, the reproductive system will follow the female pattern of development. The external genitalia will not fuse, and the

Wolffian duct system, unsupported by testosterone, will regress. In contrast, the Müllerian duct system in the absence of MIF will develop into the fallopian tubes and uterus.

4

Developmental Differences in Brain and Behavior

You have discovered that the presence or absence of specific hormones during sensitive periods in the developmental process is extremely important for the normal development of the male or female reproductive system. In this chapter, you will learn about a relatively new area of research that examines the role that hormones may have on whether the brain will develop as a female or as a male and how behavior patterns differ between the sexes.

There is no doubt that males and females differ from each other, not only physically, but behaviorally. These differences are evident from very early in the developmental process and continue throughout life. Differences between males and females are known as being **sexually dimorphic** (Figure 4.1).

Two major theories have been proposed as to how sexual dimorphism may occur. The first theory suggests that the presence of steroid hormones directs the development of the brain to be either male or female by forming pathways within the brain that are required for the control and display of sex-specific behaviors. This theory would indicate that the brain develops sexual differences in response to the presence or absence of steroid hormones just as these same hormones have been shown to control the development of sexually dimorphic genitalia. However, there is a second theory suggesting that the

Figure 4.1 The term *sexual dimorphism* explains the differences in males and females, both physically and behaviorally. Physically, males and females develop differently. Males develop muscles, body hair, and lower voices, while females develop breasts, have less body hair, and their voices do not change. Behaviorally, the more traditional view has been that girls tend to wear dresses and play with dolls, while boys play with trucks and wrestle, although many of these views are beginning to change.

influences of other individuals and one's society during the formative childhood years may result in the development of stereotypical sexual behaviors. As an example of how individuals and society might influence gender differences, take a close look at the picture of Sarah and Andrew on page 18. Although they are the same size and their hair is blond and the same length, you can easily determine that Sarah is the one wearing pink.

The influence of family and society on an individual may shape and define what one perceives as "acceptable" social behavior. Girls wear dresses, play with dolls, and have tea parties. Boys get dirty, collect frogs, and participate in rough and tumble play. The concept of gender-specific behaviors (behaviors that are traditionally exhibited by one sex more than the other) that are acceptable within a society today can and does change or evolve over time. A once non-traditional behavior can become the accepted "norm." For example, 15–20 years ago, all flight attendants on commercial airlines were women. Being a flight attendant was believed to be a female role. Today, there is no sexual bias for flight attendants. However, the concept of a male nurse still causes many people to question if they heard correctly. Although this example is oversimplified, it allows you to see how behaviors can change as attitudes change. The most obvious of the sexually dimorphic behaviors are directed toward repro-duction—patterns of behavior that bring the two sexes together at the most beneficial time to ensure a successful pregnancy and raising of their young.

For many years, research has attempted to understand the vast number of ways the brain functions. Knowing how the brain works in a normal healthy individual will allow us to better understand the working of the brain when it is considered abnormal, as in a person suffering from Parkinson's disease or Alzheimer's disease. In their attempts at deciphering many facets of how the brain functions, scientists have been extremely interested in the development of the brain during the embryonic stage as well as when the child is born and experiences societal influences.

Early in fetal development, the gonads in all embryos are initially indifferent—developing without regard to the genetic sex. This indifference holds true for the developing embryonic brain, which also begins as an indifferent organ. In the case of the developing embryonic brain, however, genetic sex does not appear to have a direct effect on whether it will develop as male or female. As you learned in Chapter 2, once the genetic sex has determined the developmental path of the gonad, the specific hormones produced by that gonad become the controlling factors in much of the remaining embryonic development.

The potential for female- or male-typical behaviors that will eventually be displayed in the adult appear to be established in the fetus by early and probably constant exposure to hormones or lack of hormones. Behavioral scientists now believe hormonal exposure, or the lack thereof, appear to be the regulating factor(s) in organizing pathways that will control sex-specific reproductive behaviors in the adult. These pathways are organized by the presence or absence of specific hormones circulating through the brain. Studies on rats have shown that many sex-specific behaviors exhibited by the adult (aggression, mating, and parental behaviors) appear to be established within the first 10 days after birth. During this 10-day period, the pathways that will control these behaviors in the adult are organized by the presence or absence of steroid hormones.

In rats, sexually dimorphic behaviors can be manipulated by either exposing animals to male-pattern androgens or keeping them free of female-pattern androgens. Also, androgen exposure must occur during a specific "sensitive period" in prenatal or **perinatal** development. The notion of a sensitive period in which hormones affect the organization of the brain was established by observations that demonstrated certain pathways developed according to a specific time table or window in development. **Masculinization** and **defeminization** of behaviors expressed by adult animals can be induced by exposure to androgens before 10 days of age. In contrast, **feminization** and **demasculinization** of adult behaviors occur when rats are not exposed to androgens in their first 10 days of life. By day 25, no amount of androgen treatment will result in masculinization.

Although somewhat controversial, research during the past decade has demonstrated that the human brain may also

(continued on page 42)

THE ORGANIZATIONAL/ACTIVATIONAL ROLE OF HORMONES

Earlier in this book, it was established that once the genetic sex of an individual is determined, hormones (specifically sex steroid hormones) are responsible for all of the remaining sexual-dimorphic characteristics and behaviors a fetus will develop. In the late 1950s, scientists became interested in the possible actions sex steroids may have on the nervous system of a developing fetus or newborn. They discovered that when a female guinea pig was exposed to testosterone prenatally, the brain became masculinized, and it failed to exhibit appropriate female reproductive behaviors later in life. This gave rise to the concept of *organizational effects*: that early exposure to androgens permanently altered the developing brain, causing it to function in a masculine or defeminized manner as an adult. In males, absence of androgens will permanently alter the brain to be feminine or demasculinized. In other words, sexual differentiation of the nervous system (and subsequent behaviors) is directed by the same steroid cues that resulted in the sexual differentiation of the body.

The effect of early hormonal exposure results in the display of sexually dimorphic behaviors in the adult. The cues for adult behaviors are referred to as *activational effects*. As an example, androgens provided in adulthood activate male copulatory behavior by stimulating the neural structures organized earlier by the same hormones. Unlike organizational effects which are permanent, activational effects of hormones on adult behavior are temporary and will decline as the hormone is broken down in the brain.

To summarize, sexually dimorphic changes resulting from the presence or absence of a specific hormone in the developing brain *organizes* the neural pathways that control certain behaviors as an adult. However, once the pathways have been established, adult behaviors can only be *activated* by the presence of the same hormone that regulated the organizational effects. Therefore, females, masculinized during development, will not exhibit female behaviors as an adult but will exhibit male behaviors if androgens are administered. Subsequently, males feminized by the absence of androgens during development do not display typical male behaviors as an adult but will display female behaviors directed by the neural pathways organized during fetal development.

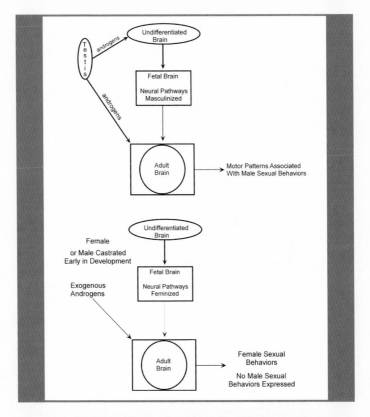

Figure 4.2 These diagrams illustrate the organizational/activational hypothesis depicting the role of hormones (or lack of hormones) on the developing brain. Androgens (upper diagram), have been found to masculinize the neural pathways and establish the brain as male. Once adulthood has been reached, androgens again play a critical role in the activation of male sexual behaviors. In the absence of androgens (lower diagram), the pathways that form in the developing brain are feminized and adult sexual behaviors are activated by estrogens.

(continued from page 39)

be organized by the presence or absence of androgens during fetal development. Exposure to androgens during a specific time during development induces the brain of the embryo to organize as a male, setting the stage for the expression of male typical behaviors as an adult. In the absence of androgens, the brain is organized in the "default mode" as female, setting the stage for the expression of female-typical behaviors as an adult. Theoretically, manipulation of the hormones that an embryo is exposed to during critical time periods in brain development could give us a biological basis to explain homosexuality.

Although specific hormones are critical for the development of the neural pathways that control sex-specific behaviors, the correct hormone is also required for the activation of these behaviors at the appropriate time and in the correct context in the adult. In the research literature, this concept is known as the Organizational/Activational Hypothesis. The organization of the pathways in the brain responsible for male-typical behavior was established by androgens during development. As an adult, these same hormones (androgens) circulating through the brain are required for the expression of male behaviors to be activated and expressed. In the female, where hormones were not required for the development of the pathways regulating female-typical behaviors, estrogen, synthesized and released by the adult ovary, has been identified as the hormone of activation that stimulates the brain to exhibit female behaviors.

CONNECTIONS

As with the development of the reproductive systems of males and females, it appears that the presence or absence of androgens may play a critical role in whether a brain is to develop as a male or female, respectively. Although the brain is said to be organized by the presence or absence of hormonal influence during prenatal or postnatal life, these same hormones have been found to activate sexual behaviors in an adult. In females, the absence of a hormonal influence results in the organization of a female brain. Later, once the female has reached maturity, elevated levels of estrogens in association with testosterone will activate sexual behavior.

5

Puberty and Beyond: Puberty in the Male

The long period of childhood, from about two to 12 years of age, is a time of continued growth of all of the systems of the body. The brain will increase to within 95% of its final size, and body weight increases to approximately 100 pounds in both sexes. Muscle strength increases, and the long bones of the arms and legs grow longer, increasing the individual's height. By the end of childhood, the body has become more like an adult's, but still sexually immature. Except for the reproductive systems of both sexes, most organ systems are now functional even though they may not have attained their adult size (Figure 5.1).

Adolescence is initiated at different times for different individuals. Females usually enter adolescence at a younger age than males. For example, in your class there will be a wide range of heights, body weights, and degrees of sexual maturity. There are always a few people who will begin their growth spurt sooner than others. Occasionally the girls will be, on average, taller than the boys. There also may be one or two individuals who still look like they are 12 years old, and there may be individuals who look much older than their age.

Once an individual enters adolescence, both the skeletal and muscular systems grow faster than at any other time in that

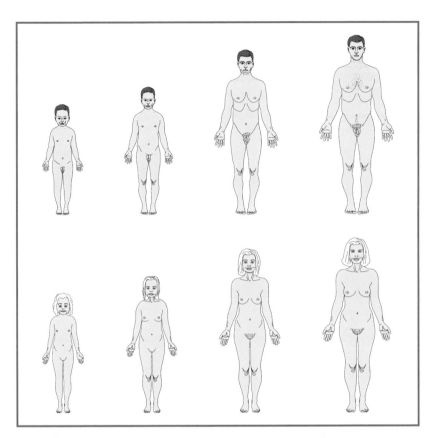

Figure 5.1 This diagram depicts the morphological changes that occur as males and females mature from childhood through puberty and into adulthood. As the female and male mature, the basic form of the body changes as secondary sexual characteristics, influenced by the production of sex hormones at puberty, affect each person's shape and size.

individual's life. The lungs will more than double in mass. Thus, Sarah and Andrew will probably not begin puberty and complete the transformation to adulthood at the same time. During adolescence, **puberty** is marked by the maturation of the reproductive system and the initiation of human sexual response. Puberty is a time when all of the **physiological**, **morphological**, and behavioral changes will occur as a girl or boy completes the final phase of maturation and becomes an adult.

In males, an indication that sexual maturation has been initiated is the occurrence of the first **ejaculation**. It may be difficult to determine an exact date for the beginning of maturity because the first ejaculation often occurs during sleep (nocturnal emission). Ejaculation, however, does not signify fertility. Before sexual maturation is complete, the ejaculate usually consists of a small quantity of seminal fluid lacking spermatozoa. However, puberty involves much more than just sexual activity. As sex hormones begin to increase in Andrew's circulation, he will notice changes in his body, his voice, and his attitude. These changes occur because of several reasons.

As explained in Chapter 3, in males, germ cells enter the genital ridge early in development and proliferate (increase) by the process of mitosis throughout embryonic life. This proliferation creates a large pool of dedicated stem cells, now called spermatogonia (singular: spermatogonium), which will produce sperm (through the process of meiosis) continuously during the male's entire adult life.

During embryonic life, the level of androgens in the blood is relatively high. This elevated concentration remains until shortly after birth. At birth, the level drops to an extremely low level and remains low until puberty is initiated between 10 and 15 years of age. During childhood and early adolescence, the testes are essentially inactive except for the synthesis of a small amount of androgens. What is extremely interesting is the fact that the male reproductive system can be fully functional at birth if the regulating hormones are present. One theory as to why spermatogenesis is not initiated immediately after the birth of a male child is due to a small area within the brain called the **hypothalamus** that has not yet matured. This region has been called the master control because it appears to control many of the body's functions, including reproduction (Figure 5.2). Also, the neural circuitry that will ultimately be responsible for the regulation of

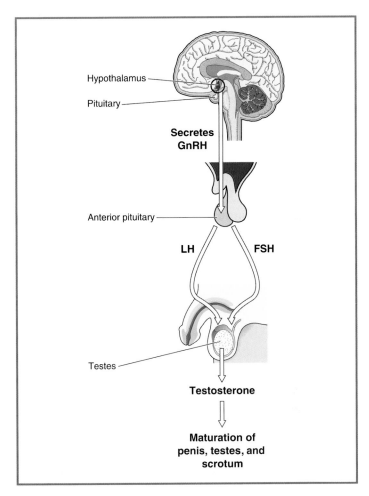

Figure 5.2 The neural regulation of the hormonal pathway resulting in testosterone production is illustrated here. At puberty, the neural-hormonal pathway regulating the synthesis and release of testosterone is dependent on the maturation and directions of the hypothalamus. Gonadotropin-releasing hormones (GnRH), synthesized in the hypothalamus, are delivered to the anterior pituitary via the hypothalamic-hypophyseal portal system. GnRH stimulates the pituitary gland to synthesize two gonadotropins, follicle stimulating hormone (FSH), and luteinizing hormone (LH). Released into the general circulation, FSH and LH are delivered to their target organs, the testes, stimulating the synthesis and release of testosterone, and controlling the development of sperm and maturation of primary sex characteristics.

reproductive events is not fully active until puberty. In addition, the hypothalamus of an immature male is extremely
sensitive to **gonadotropins**. This sensitivity to low levels of
androgens keeps the hypothalamus inactive through the
method of **negative feedback** and restricts the initiation of
spermatogenesis prior to puberty. As a male child enters
adolescence, the hypothalamus matures and, together with
the neural circuitry, loses its sensitivity to the low levels of
testosterone and gonadotropins. With this loss of sensitivity,
the negative feedback ends. The hypothalamus begins to
secrete **gonadotropin releasing hormone** (GnRH) into the
hypothalamic-hypophyseal portal system, a vascular
network that allows the hypothalamus to deliver releasing
hormones directly to the anterior pituitary gland. Once in the
pituitary gland, GnRH stimulates specific cell populations to
synthesize and release two gonadotropins, **luteinizing hormone**
(LH) and **follicle stimulating hormone** (FSH). Once
released by the anterior pituitary, LH and FSH enter the
general circulation to reach their **target tissue**, the testes.
In the testes, LH and FSH stimulate the interstitial cells of
Leydig, inactive since birth, to begin synthesizing testosterone.
Stimulated by the presence of testosterone, primary sex
characteristics such as the penis, testes, and scrotum grow
larger. Also at this time, the testes initiate the production of
sperm within the seminiferous tubules.

The seminiferous tubules are tightly coiled structures
contained in 250–300 compartments within the testes.
Between the tubules are blood vessels and the interstitial cells
of Leydig. The seminiferous tubules make up nearly 80%
of the bulk of the testes in an adult with each tubule ranging
from 0.3–1 meter in length. If placed end to end, the entire
length of seminiferous tubules would stretch for approximately
two and a half football fields.

The seminiferous tubules are composed of two cell types: the
Sertoli cells and the **spermatocytes**, which after the initiation

of puberty can be seen in various stages of sperm development throughout the remainder of the male's life. Sertoli cells are large cells that extend from the basement membrane (basal lamina) of the tubule to the center **lumen**. These cells are also referred to as nurse cells because one of their functions is to protect and nurse (take care of) sperm as they develop. The Sertoli cells are linked (fused) to each other by **tight junctions**, and the basement membrane forms a barrier preventing unwanted and possibly toxic substances from entering the tubule. Tight junctions are also referred to as the **blood-testis barrier** and are very efficient at preventing large molecules and interstitial fluids from entering the tubules.

Sperm production, initiated at puberty, is from that point on, continuous throughout the male's adult life. Spermatogonia (containing 46 chromosomes) are clustered just inside the basement membrane of the seminiferous tubule between adjacent Sertoli cells. Some of the spermatogonia will remain in this area near the basement membrane as reserve cells. They will continue to produce spermatogonia via mitosis for the rest of the individual's life. Other spermatogonia enter meiosis and become primary spermatocytes, the first step in sperm cell development. The development and maturation of primary spermatocytes takes approximately 22 days and represents the longest developmental period of the spermatogenic cycle. Because of this rather lengthy period of development, the majority of cells visible under the microscope will be primary spermatocytes.

At the completion of the first meiotic division, the smaller, secondary spermatocytes are produced. These secondary spermatocytes contain 23 chromosomes, but have twice the amount of DNA, indicating that the chromosomes are paired with their copy. The secondary spermatocyte period of sperm development is relatively brief and is usually hard to identify because they enter the second meiotic division almost immediately. Because secondary spermatocytes begin the second meiotic division so rapidly, no DNA replication has occurred. The second meiotic division then results in the production of spermatids containing 23 chromosomes with only half the DNA. The two-phase meiotic process, therefore, results in the formation of spermatids that contain only half the number of chromosomes (haploid) of the original spermatogonia.

Spermatids now undergo **spermiogenesis**, a complex process of cellular changes that convert a small round cell into a smaller mobile cell. These changes encompass the formation of an **acrosome**, development of a flagellum, and condensation and elongation of the nucleus, closely associated with the dramatic reduction of the cytoplasm. Making the cell more streamlined, gaining a mode of propulsion, and losing the weight of excess cytoplasm creates and greatly enhances sperm mobility (Figure 5.3). Once the sperm reaches the egg, the acrosome becomes critical because it contains enzymes needed to penetrate the outer layers of the egg, deliver the sperm's chromosomes, and initiate cellular division. The acrosome is also responsible for inducing the **acrosomal reaction**, preventing the entrance of additional sperm. The end result of spermatogenesis is the production of mature sperm that are released into the lumen of the seminiferous tubule in a process called **spermiation.**

Hormonal control of spermatogenesis follows the pathway that was described earlier in this chapter. Gonadotropin releasing hormone from the hypothalamus regulates the synthesis and release of LH and FSH from the anterior pituitary. This gland, in turn, stimulates the production of testosterone by the interstitial cells of Leydig found in the testes.

The actual target of FSH within the testes is the Sertoli cells. FSH stimulates Sertoli cells to secrete a chemical substance that is needed for the sustained mitotic divisions of spermatogonia and to aid in the process of spermatogenesis. Unlike other hormones involved in the production of sperm, FSH levels are

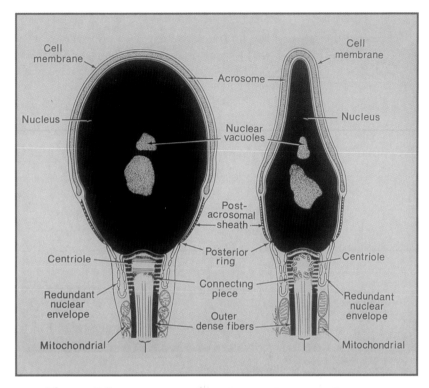

Figure 5.3 Pictured here is a diagram of a mammalian sperm undergoing spermiogenesis. The acrosome and flagellum form, the nucleus condenses and elongates, and the cell becomes more streamlined, ready to travel through the female's uterus in search of an egg to fertilize.

not closely regulated by the hypothalamus. The Sertoli cells have been found to produce two chemicals, inhibin and activin, which appear to play large role in regulating FSH concentrations.

The primary target of LH is the interstitial cells of Leydig that are stimulated by the elevated levels of LH to synthesize and secrete testosterone into the seminiferous tubules and general circulation. The release of testosterone completes a feedback pathway that, at high concentrations, will inhibit LH production by the anterior pituitary.

Testosterone, FSH, and LH are essential for spermatogenesis because they are required for testosterone synthesis. Spermatogenesis is a very difficult process to examine. Variations observed in animal models may not accurately reflect the process as it occurs in humans. In fact, it may take a long time before the way testosterone and FSH are involved in the regulation of spermatogenesis can be determined.

The development of spermatozoa from the division of spermatogonia to the release of mature sperm takes approximately 64 days. Different regions of the seminiferous tubule contain varying stages of spermatocyte development. Staggering developmental stages allows sperm production to remain essentially constant. Approximately 200 million sperm are produced every day. That may seem to be a large number, but it is actually only about the number of sperm released during a single ejaculation.

Sperm released into the lumen of the seminiferous tubules (Figure 5.4) are not yet mature and do not have the ability to swim. Immature sperm are pushed out of the seminiferous tubules by other sperm and the fluids produced by the Sertoli cells. As sperm enter the epididymis, they complete maturation, stimulated in part by protein secretions from the epididymal cells during the 12 days it takes to move through the ducts. Even after all the time and manipulation required to produce mature sperm, ejaculated sperm are not yet capable of fertilizing an egg. Ejaculated sperm must depend on secretions found in the female reproductive tract to initiate fertility in a process called capacitation.

When sperm leave the vas deferens during ejaculation, they combine with fluids that are secreted from several accessory glands. This sperm-fluid mixture is known as **semen**. Approximately 99% of the volume of semen is fluid added from the bulbourethral glands, seminal vesicles, and the prostate gland. Semen provides a liquid medium for sperm delivery. It includes buffers that are needed to neutralize the acidic

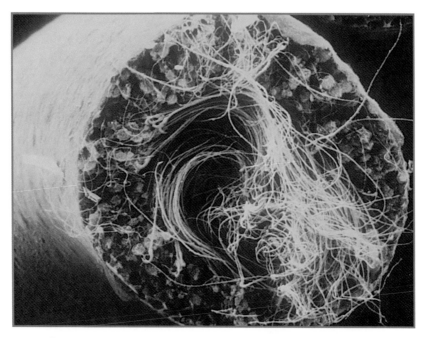

Figure 5.4 This scanning electron micrograph of a cross section of a seminiferous tubule shows the various stages of spermatogenesis. Spermatogonia are located next to the basal lamina where they proliferate by mitosis and a portion of these cells begin the process of spermatogenesis. As spermatogenesis progresses, cells move toward the lumen of the seminiferous tubule where, once formed, the sperm are released into the lumen and may pass out of the body during ejaculation.

environment of the vagina, nutrients for sperm metabolism, and mucous for lubrication. In addition, the seminal vesicles secrete **prostaglandins** that appear to influence sperm motility and transport in both the male and female reproductive tracts. One very interesting component of semen is zinc. Although the role of zinc is unclear, low concentrations have been associated with male infertility.

In addition to spermatogenesis, androgens influence a number of changes in the body as the child matures into an adult. Previously, the primary sexual characteristics were identified as the visible male genitalia: the penis, scrotum, and testicles. At puberty, these structures respond to the stimulation of elevated levels of testosterone (or androgens) and go through a period of growth. Secondary sex characteristics are physical features that respond to the increased level of circulating androgens in males and estrogens in females. Most of these characteristics are not directly related to or

THINK ABOUT THIS:

Impotence affects between 10–15 million men in the United States. Impotence is more clinically defined as the inability to attain or maintain an erection allowing for sexual intercourse (erectile dysfunction). Erectile dysfunction (ED) most often results from damage to vascular or connective tissues in the penis due to the normal aging process. Other causes can include damage to spinal nerves controlling blood flow to the penis, endocrine dysfunction (lack of testosterone), or diseases such as kidney disorders, atherosclerosis, and diabetes mellitus. Erectile dysfunction increases with age and is also exacerbated by smoking, alcohol, and drug use (both prescription and illegal). However, ED does not require a physical basis, and it has been estimated that 10–20% of all cases are purely psychological. Feelings of stress, depression, anxiety, and guilt are all known to increase the incidence of ED.

Treatments for ED may include oral testosterone replacement (provided testosterone is the primary problem) and an injection of specific drugs directly into the penis. Other treatments may include surgery to rebuild damaged arteries or the insertion of a prosthetic device that can produce an erection. In recent years, a drug called Viagra® has changed the outlook of men suffering from ED. Viagra® works by mimicking the effects of nitric oxide which induces arterial dilation in the penis. Relaxation of the arterial smooth muscle increases the blood flow to the erectile tissues, resulting in an erection.

involved in reproduction. As Andrew matures, his body will undergo many changes in response to an increase of circulating androgens, reshaping his body to that of an adult. Male secondary sex characteristics include such things as a thickening of the vocal cords which effectively lowers the voice, increases in the thickness of the skin, muscle development, bone size and density, as well as experiencing an increased sex drive or libido. Androgens also stimulate the growth of facial, pubic, and underarm hair. These same androgens can be responsible for increased body hair and the loss of hair on the head many years later.

CONNECTIONS

As puberty begins, a region in the brain called the hypothalamus matures and directs the neural pathways to begin releasing GnRH. This hormone stimulates the anterior pituitary to release gonadotropins, which, in turn, stimulate the testes to secrete testosterone. As the hormone pathway develops, the testes initiate spermatogenesis, and the male reproductive system begins to mature. Increases in the secretion of testosterone stimulate the development of primary and secondary sex characteristics, further demonstrating that maturation is occurring.

6

Puberty and Beyond: Puberty in the Female

Puberty in females is defined by the onset of the **menstrual cycle (menarche)**, which usually occurs between 9–15 years of age. Genetics may play a part in the age at which menarche occurs. For example, if Sarah's mother began puberty at a relatively young age, it might be an indication that she will also enter puberty at a young age. As in the male, scientists have worked for years hoping to identify the event or series of events that trigger the beginning of puberty. However, they have not been able to form any definitive conclusions. From these studies, scientists have been able to accumulate a vast understanding of the sequence of events that occurs between the initiation of puberty and sexual maturation.

In Chapter 2, you read how the ovaries develop and that all of the **oocytes** (eggs) that the ovary will ever contain are produced before birth. In the first 3–5 weeks of fetal life, approximately 2,000 germ cells migrate to the genital ridges. These stem cells, now called **oogonia**, invade the cortex of the developing ovary and start proliferating by active mitosis. By week 8 postconception, their number has increased to approximately 600,000. Between 8–13 weeks, some of the oogonia stop mitosis and begin the first meiotic division. In those cells that did not enter meiosis, mitotic division continues until about the fifth or sixth month. At this time, the fetal ovary contains between 6–7 million oogonia that have all started meiosis and are now classified as primary oocytes. From this point on, the number of primary oocytes declines significantly so that at birth, only 1–2 million remain. This marked decline is caused by a process called **atresia** in which the primary oocytes degenerate and are reabsorbed by the surrounding ovarian tissues. It appears that the survival of an oocyte in the fetal ovary is highly dependent on its association and encapsulation by the surrounding granulosa cells. The number of oocytes will continue to decline with increasing age. By the beginning of puberty, only about 400,000 oocytes remain in the ovary. However, only about 450 eggs will ovulate during a woman's reproductive years.

The process of meiosis in the oocyte is a very protracted event that can last for many years. Midway through fetal development, all of the oogonia (now classified as oocytes) initiate meiosis and advance to the prophase stage of the first meiotic division (Prophase I). The primary oocytes will then remain suspended at this stage until they are ovulated, anywhere from 13 to more than 50 years later, ending at menopause. The mechanisms regulating the initiation of meiosis and the prolonged period of arrest are not very well understood. What is known, however, is that the presence of two X chromosomes seems to be required for the oocyte to not only enter meiosis, but also to survive the long period of time it is suspended at prophase I. Resumption of meiosis will occur just before ovulation. This topic will be covered later in the chapter during a discussion of the menstrual cycle.

During childhood and early adolescence, Sarah's blood will contain low levels of estrogen. Estrogen, like testosterone in males, is the end product of a chemical pathway that began in the area of the brain called the hypothalamus. The hypothalamus acts as a master control center, regulating any number of physiological events such as hormone regulation, water and chemical balance, and regulation of body temperature. One of those events is the regulation of reproductive activity, from puberty and beyond. Just as you discovered in males, in

prepubescent females, the hypothalamus appears to be extremely sensitive to the circulating sex steroid, estrogen. Therefore, the presence of low levels of estrogen in Sarah's blood before the beginning of puberty has an inhibitory (negative feedback) effect on the hypothalamus and essentially keeps it shut off. These low levels of estrogen keep the hypothalamus from sending the chemical signal, GnRH, to the anterior pituitary and initiating puberty.

As stated earlier, the signal, cue, or events that initiate sexual development are not known. As in males, the initiation of puberty in females may also be dependent on the maturation of the hypothalamus. In addition, most of the chemical signals generated by the hypothalamus are sent to the pituitary gland which has been found to control so many vital functions concerning the overall well-being of the body or homeostasis. It is referred to as the "master gland." Not only does the hypothalamus need to mature before the onset of puberty, but the communication network, the hypothalamic-hypophyseal portal system, must also be established.

As the hypothalamus matures and takes control of Sarah's reproductive life, low levels of estrogen are now stimulatory to the hypothalamus initiating the production of estrogen. GnRH, which is produced by neurons in the hypothalamus, is released into the hypothalamic-hypophyseal portal system and transported directly to the cells of the anterior pituitary gland. GnRH stimulates cells in the anterior pituitary gland that produce the gonadotropins LH and FSH. This hormonal pathway is the exact same pathway that was described in the male. LH and FSH were originally discovered in females, so when the same hormones were found in males, the female related names were kept. LH, stimulated by the release of gonadotropin releasing hormones (GnRH) from the hypothalamus, is delivered to the ovaries where LH stimulates the granulosa cells of the primary follicle (target tissue) to synthesize and secrete estrogen. The estrogen produced by the granulosa cells can be utilized in the ovary or released into the circulation, affecting other reproductive functions and structures. In response to elevated levels of estrogen in the circulation, Sarah's body will go through a number of changes to initiate her first menstrual cycle.

In females, estrogen controls the development of primary sex characteristics, just as androgen controls the development of these characteristics in males. However, development of secondary sex characteristics in females requires both estrogen and androgens. Estrogen controls the most prominent of the secondary sex traits—the female pattern of fat distribution on the hips and upper thighs, and the development of the breasts. Other female secondary sex characteristics such as pubic and axillary (armpit) hair growth and libido are actually under the control of androgens produced by the **adrenal cortex**.

Unlike the male cycle that, once initiated, is continuous throughout the remainder of the life of the male, maturation and release of gametes in the female are cyclic, occurring approximately once a month. This cycle is commonly called the menstrual cycle (Figure 6.1), taking an average of 28 days to complete (the normal range is 24–35 days). The menstrual cycle can be described by the sequence of hormonal and morphological changes occurring in the ovary (ovarian cycle) and the **endometrial lining** of the uterus (uterine cycle).

The ovarian cycle, regulated by the pituitary gonadotropins LH and FSH, is divided into three phases: the follicular phase, ovulation, and the luteal phase. The uterine cycle, regulated by the ovarian hormones, estrogen, and progesterone, can also be divided into three phases: menses, the proliferative phase, and the secretory phase. Ultimately, the ovarian cycle is initiated producing the estrogen and progesterone that control and regulate the uterine cycle. Although the uterine cycle is dependent on the ovarian cycle, both the ovarian and uterine cycles occur within the same time period and end at the time of menstrual flow. Although the menstrual cycle is essentially a continuous process, we will examine it in stages.

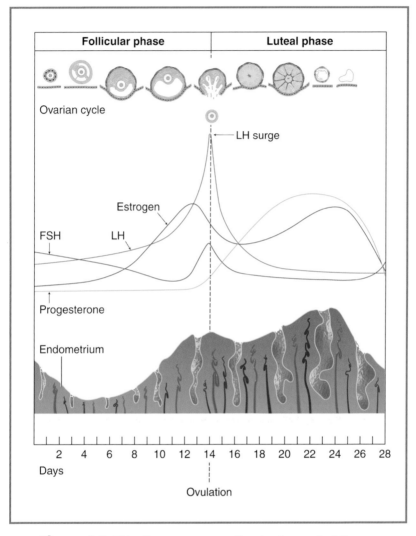

Figure 6.1 This diagram compares the development of the egg and uterine lining as they are associated with pituitary and ovarian hormones. As the egg is preparing to leave the follicle, estrogen and LH levels rise while FSH remains constant. Just before the egg is released, LH levels surge. At this point, the uterine lining is very thick, ready to provide nutrients for a fertilized egg. If the egg is not fertilized, progesterone levels rise, the egg is expelled from the body, and the uterine lining is released through the process of menstruation.

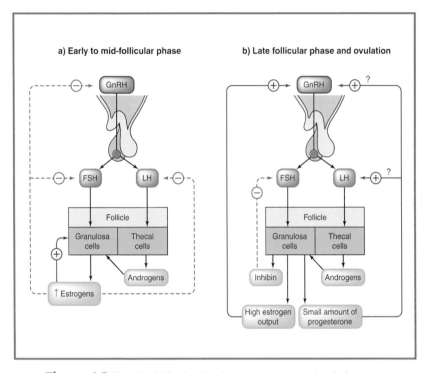

a) Early to mid-follicular phase

b) Late follicular phase and ovulation

Figure 6.2 Early in follicular development, estrogen levels increase to a moderate level. This increase in estrogen has an inhibitory effect on both the hypothalamus and pituitary, lowering the levels of FSH and LH. In the late follicular phase, estrogen levels are high and have an excitatory effect on the hypothalamus, increasing the estrogen even further. This dramatic increase in estrogen levels results in ovulation.

THE FOLLICULAR AND PROLIFERATIVE PHASE

Because follicular development is the major event at the beginning of the menstrual cycle, it has been labeled the *follicular phase* (Figure 6.2). This phase can be the most variable in length, lasting anywhere from 10 days to three weeks.

Day 1 of the menstrual cycle is identified as the first day of menstruation. This point was chosen because it is an easily monitored physical sign. Menses, when the endometrial lining of the uterus is sloughed off as the menstrual flow, is the first phase of the uterine cycle and lasts on the average of 4–5 days.

The sloughing of the uterine lining occurs in response to the decline of progesterone and estrogen that is necessary for the maintenance of the uterine lining. Immediately before the beginning of each menstrual cycle, the negative feedback of progesterone on the hypothalamus ends as progesterone levels decline and the hypothalamus can then again release GnRH. This stimulates the anterior pituitary to increase its release of gonadotropins.

In the presence of FSH, several follicles in the ovary begin to mature. Why some follicles will develop and ovulate, while others develop but do not ovulate, and still others will not

ESTROGEN: IT CAN DO A BODY GOOD

Much of this book has examined differences in the reproductive physiology of males and females. However, not all differences between the sexes are as obvious as morphological characteristics. In particular, the incidence of cardiovascular disease is dramatically different between men and women. This is important because more people in the United States die from cardiovascular disease than from all other causes of death combined. However, men are four times more likely to suffer from some type of cardiovascular disease than women and are 40 times more likely to suffer a heart attack.

Scientists believe the above facts suggest that something protects women from cardiovascular problems. However, it is also well established that this "cardiovascular protection" does not continue throughout the female's entire life. Once women reach their mid-40s (the age at which most women experience menopause), they begin to suffer from cardiovascular disease at an accelerated rate and by the time they reach 70, they experience cardiovascular disease and heart attacks at the same rate as men of the same age. In fact, clinical studies have shown that premenopausal women have a lower incidence of cardiovascular disease than postmenopausal women.

develop at all remains a mystery. Some scientists theorize that follicles closer to the blood supply may be stimulated to a greater extent than those farther removed from circulation. As the follicles grow, the shell of granulosa cells under the influence of FSH and the thecal cells forming the outermost layer of the follicle produce steroid hormones under the control of LH. This outer layer of **thecal** cells synthesize androgens that are secreted into the granulosa cells where an enzyme converts them to estrogen.

As estrogen increases in the circulation, several things happen. Estrogen exerts a negative feedback on pituitary FSH

Physiologists now believe that estrogen may in some way protect women from cardiovascular problems. Recently, research has demonstrated that estrogen, at premenopausal levels, stimulates the production of nitric oxide in the endothelial cells (lining) of arteries, including those in the heart. Nitric oxide is one of the most important vascular regulatory agents in the body, capable of relaxing the smooth muscle surrounding arteries. Many drugs, natural occurring hormones, and neuro- transmitters in our bodies can relax arteries by stimulating the production of nitric oxide. Coronary arteries relax to a greater extent in response to drugs and naturally occurring agents when normal levels of estrogen are present because estrogen increases their ability to stimulate nitric oxide production. This increased response to estrogen has been suggested as the factor that lowers the incident of cardiovascular disease in females.

In England, the importance of estrogen and cardiac health has been taken to the next level. Ambulances in England now carry injectable estrogen and administer it to patients (male or female) who are suffering symptoms of heart attack.

and LH secretions, preventing the development and maturation of any follicles during the current cycle. At the same time, circulating estrogens act as a **positive feedback**, stimulating the granulosa cells to produce more estrogen even though FSH and LH levels have been reduced. As the follicles continue to grow, a cavity called the antrum forms and is filled with fluid secreted by the granulosa cells. This fluid contains hormones and enzymes that will be used at ovulation. At some time during the follicular phase, some of the developing follicles suffer a hormone regulated cell death and will undergo atresia. By the time ovulation occurs, usually only one dominant follicle remains. However, as described earlier, fraternal twins like Sarah and Andrew are the result of two eggs ovulating during the same menstrual cycle.

In the uterus, menstruation has ended. Under the stimulatory influence of circulating estrogens, the *proliferative phase* begins. This phase is characterized by an increased blood supply, bringing nutrients and oxygen to the dramatically increased number of cells that make up the developing endometrial layer.

As the follicular phase ends, estrogen secretion is at a maximum level and the granulosa cells of the dominant follicle begin to produce inhibin and progesterone. Earlier in the follicular phase, low levels of estrogen exerted an inhibitory effect or negative feedback on the release of GnRH and gonadotropins. Now at these elevated levels, estrogen becomes stimulatory or a positive feedback and, along with the elevated levels of progesterone, increases the sensitivity of the pituitary gland to GnRH. This causes a dramatic increase in LH secretion, an event known as the LH surge. FSH, which is no longer needed, also surges, but to a lesser degree, probably due to the influence of inhibin.

The LH surge is required for the follicle to continue toward ovulation. In the absence of LH, the final events of oocyte maturation cannot take place. However, due to the LH surge, meiosis, halted in the egg, resumes, completing the first meiotic division. This first division converts the primary oocyte, contained within the dominate follicle, into a secondary **oocyte** and a **polar body**. Formation of polar bodies during maturation of the egg is a method that removes the extra chromosomes but leaves the products accumulated within the cell that, if pregnancy occurs, will support the fertilized egg until the placenta is operational. The LH surge also stimulates the granulosa cells to continue dividing as the size of the follicle increases and rapidly accumulate additional fluid within the antrum in preparation for release of the egg.

Elevated estrogen in the later portion of the follicular phase stimulates the endometrial lining of the uterus to grow to a final thickness of 3–4 milimeters in anticipation of pregnancy as the proliferative phase comes to an end. Just before ovulation, the cervical glands produce large amounts of mucus to facilitate sperm entry.

OVULATION

Sixteen–24 hours after the levels of the hormones rise, *ovulation* (Figure 6.3) occurs. At this time, the mature follicle secretes **collagenase**, an **enzyme** that dissolves **collagen** in the tissue that binds the follicular cells to each other. The remains of the dissolving collagen result in an **inflammatory reaction** causing white blood cells to release prostaglandins into the follicle. Although prostaglandins are not completely understood, scientists have suggested that they stimulate smooth muscle cells to contract, rupturing the follicle and ejecting the antral fluid that contains the egg, still covered with 3–4 layers of granulosa cells. The egg is swept into the fallopian tube where it will be fertilized or, if not fertilized, will be broken down and reabsorbed by the lining of the oviduct.

After the rupture of the follicle, thecal cells under the

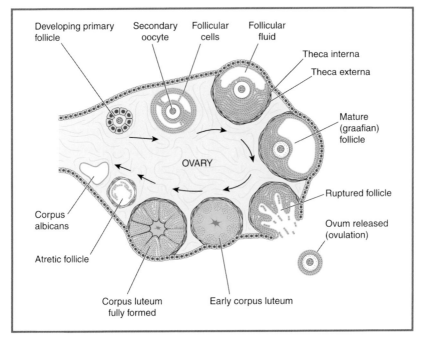

Developing primary follicle

Secondary oocyte

Follicular cells

Follicular fluid

Theca interna

Theca externa

Mature (graafian) follicle

OVARY

Ruptured follicle

Ovum released (ovulation)

Corpus albicans

Atretic follicle

Corpus luteum fully formed

Early corpus luteum

Figure 6.3 This diagram presents the various stages of follicular development that leads to ovulation and the development of the corpus luteum. As a primary follicle begins to mature, there is an increase in the ovum and the surrounding follicular cells. As the follicle grows, it develops two layers covering its outer surface. The thecal cells stimulated by FSH secrete testosterone and the granulosa cells in response to LH secrete estrogen. When the mature (graafian) follicle ruptures, the granulosa/follicle cells remaining in the ovary form the corpus luteum that secretes both estrogen and progesterone. If pregnancy occurs, the corpus luteum will continue to function as an endocrine gland for the entire pregnancy. If pregnancy does not occur, the corpus luteum will remain active for approximately 14 days at which time it will degenerate, forming a small white scar on the surface of the ovary called a corpus albicans.

control of LH migrate into the antral space containing the remaining granulosa cells. Both cell types transform into luteal cells of the corpus luteum. The luteal cells accumulate lipids in their cytoplasm and begin to secrete a high concentration of progesterone and a moderate level of estrogen from these transformed cells.

THE LUTEAL AND SECRETORY PHASE

After ovulation, the corpus luteum produces increasing amounts of progesterone and estrogen. Progesterone becomes the dominant hormone. Although estrogen levels increase moderately, they never reach the preovulatory levels. This cocktail of estrogen and progesterone exerts a negative feedback on the hypothalamus and, with the help of inhibin, the anterior pituitary gland. This negative feedback essentially shuts off GnRH production by the hypothalamus and gonadotropin release from the anterior pituitary, effectively blocking the ovary from initiating follicle development.

Progesterone continues to stimulate the endometrium of the uterus stimulating the secretory phase as it prepares for pregnancy. The number of blood vessels in the uterine lining increases and the uterine glands enlarge and become highly coiled, significantly increasing the size and surface area of each gland. The cells of the uterine glands begin to store lipids and glycogen in their cytoplasm to supply nutrients to the developing embryo while the **placenta** is developing. Also in response to progesterone, the cervical mucus thickens to form a plug that blocks the cervical opening from invading bacteria and additional sperm.

If pregnancy does not occur, the corpus luteum will cease to function after about 12 days. The corpus luteum degenerates into an inactive structure called the **corpus albicans**. As the luteal cells degenerate, progesterone and estrogen levels decrease. This decrease removes the negative feedback signal to the hypothalamus and anterior pituitary gland, and secretion of GnRH, LH, and FSH resumes.

The secretory endothelium is dependent on progesterone for continued maintenance. When the corpus luteum degenerates and hormone production has ended, blood vessels supplying the surface layer of the endothelium constrict, shutting off oxygen and nutrients. Without oxygen and nutrients, the cells of the endometrial lining begin to die and approximately 14 days after ovulation, the endometrial layer begins to slough off as the menstrual flow begins once again.

CONNECTIONS

Initiation of puberty in the female, like the male, requires the maturation of the hypothalamus, pituitary gland, and the connections by which they communicate. In addition, the sensitivity of the hypothalamus to low levels of estrogen is reduced, allowing for the release of GnRH stimulating the anterior pituitary gland to synthesize and release gonadotropins. The gonadotropins (LH and FSH) are released into the general circulation and delivered to the ovary where they stimulate the production of estrogen. Initiation of puberty in females, on average, is several years earlier than in males. However, researchers still have no idea as to when and why puberty is initiated in each individual.

The reproductive cycle that is established in the female is a little more complicated than the male reproductive cycle. In females, hormone concentrations are modified over a 28–36 day period called the menstrual cycle. During each cycle, several follicles and the ova they contain begin to mature and at the same time, hormonal changes prepare the uterus for the possibility of accepting a fertilized egg and the development of a fetus. During the follicular phase of the menstrual cycle, the selected follicles grow and release greater amounts of estrogen into the circulation. This increase in estrogen causes a negative feedback where the hypothalamus decreases the secretion of GnRH affecting the release of LH and FSH from the anterior pituitary. This temporary reduction in LH and FSH usually results in the selection of only one follicle that continues to develop and ovulate. Immediately prior to ovulation, meiosis, dormant since before birth, resumes.

Once ovulation occurs, the follicle cells that housed the ovum remain as part of the ovary and metamorphose into an endocrine structure called the corpus luteum. This begins the luteal phase of the menstrual cycle in which progesterone becomes the controlling hormone and, in association with estrogen, continues to prepare the uterus to accept a fertilized ovum. If pregnancy occurs, the high levels of progesterone will effectively stop the secretion of GnRH so that no more ova will initiate development during the pregnancy. If pregnancy does not occur, the corpus luteum will continue functioning for about two weeks. Without the support of the hormones from the corpus luteum, the hypothalamus resumes secretion of GnRH, and the uterine lining sloughs off as the menstrual flow. The cycle begins again.

7

Concerns and Complications

Getting pregnant is not difficult to achieve if both partners are healthy. In fact, the annual pregnancy rate without any form of birth control is between 85 and 95%. Additionally, timing may improve the odds of pregnancy. For example, a couple trying to conceive might choose to have intercourse in the middle of the menstrual cycle around the time ovulation occurs.

INFERTILITY

However, for some couples, getting pregnant is relatively difficult if not entirely impossible. A couple is considered **infertile** if they have not been able to conceive after a year of trying. Approximately 15% of all couples in the United States fit into this category. Infertility can be attributed equally to both men and women.

Infertility in males is usually the result of a low number of normal healthy sperm. The chance that any one sperm will reach and fertilize an egg is extremely low even in a normal male with approximately 200 million sperm per ejaculation. Therefore, a male with a sperm count below 55–60 million per ejaculation would be considered, for all practical purposes, infertile. Remedying a low sperm count may be as simple as changing the style of underwear the man wears, or the size of his pants, both of which might cause the testes to be maintained at too high of a temperature. The optimal temperature for sperm development is roughly 4° C lower than body temperature. The scrotum is a relatively unique structure that can move the testes closer to or away from the body, effectively controlling testicular temperature. Switching from tight briefs and pants that may hold the testes too close to the body to boxers and looser pants may increase a man's sperm count. Other conditions that result in a low sperm count may not be as easy to correct. Low testosterone levels, immune disorders that attack sperm, radiation, drugs such as anabolic steroids and marijuana, and diseases such as mumps and gonorrhea, may all contribute to male infertility.

The causes related to female infertility are much more variable. Irregular menstrual cycles can make it hard to time ovulation and determine the optimal time for conception. Abnormal production of LH and FSH may disrupt the production of follicles and ovulation. One of the most common causes of infertility is pelvic inflammatory disease (PID), a general term for any severe bacterial infection of the female reproductive tract. PID that reaches the oviducts can cause scarring that may seal the oviducts and prevent passage of the egg or sperm. PID can be overcome in approximately 25% of all cases by a surgical procedure that opens the oviduct. The strongly acidic vaginal secretions or a thick mucus of some women can damage sperm and make it difficult to move toward the egg. Endometriosis, found in 1–3% of women, is a condition in which the endometrial tissue (lining of the uterus) migrates up the oviduct and implants on organs such as the bladder, kidneys, ovaries, and the colon. This misplaced tissue is stimulated each month by the hormonal cycle and can cause pain and infertility. Endometriosis can sometimes be corrected by surgery, drugs, or hormonal therapy.

Failure of a fertile couple to achieve reproductive success can, in many instances, be attributed to spontaneous abortion, or miscarriage. A miscarriage is defined as the loss of a fetus before it develops sufficiently to survive outside the uterus. Studies have estimated that as many as one-third of all pregnancies end in miscarriages, some occurring so early in the pregnancy that the woman was unaware that she had even conceived.

The reproductive success of females is affected by age much more than in males. By her mid-40s, a woman's ovaries contain far fewer oocytes and become less responsive to LH and FSH. Also, oocytes ovulated near the end of a woman's reproductive life are more likely to have been damaged by years of exposure to toxins in our environment as well as radiation, drugs, chemicals, and disease.

INCREASING FERTILITY

Modern techniques are now available to help infertile couples conceive. Many of these techniques did not exist even a decade ago. There are no guarantees of success, and the techniques can be very expensive. Some couples have been known to spend in excess of $250,000 in the hope of becoming biological parents. These techniques include fertility-enhancing drugs, artificial insemination, *in vitro* fertilization (IVF), and gamete intra-fallopian transfer (GIFT). If all else fails, some couples may hire a surrogate mother.

Fertility-enhancing drugs increase the production of developing eggs. These drugs are given to enhance a couple's chances of conceiving by natural means. In many cases, these drugs are given to women preparing for IVF so many eggs can be collected during one harvesting procedure. Occasionally, multiple pregnancies occur as a result of these medications. Births of four or more babies in one pregnancy almost certainly are influenced by fertility-enhancing drugs.

Artificial insemination is the most common, least expensive, and easiest technique to enhance reproductive success. This method can be used when a man's sperm count is low. Sperm are collected over an extended period of time, accumulating an amount of active sperm that would be equal to the number found in a normal ejaculation. Using a syringe, all of the collected sperm are placed into the uterus as close to the time of ovulation as possible. Artificial insemination is also a viable option for men who produce no sperm. In this case the woman may receive anonymously donated sperm from a "sperm bank" to fertilize her egg. Also, for a single woman who wishes to become a parent, artificial insemination is a very feasible alternative. Each year in the United States, more than 25,000 births are the result of artificial insemination.

In vitro fertilization (IVF) is defined as "fertilization in a test tube" (Figure 7.1). The first child produced by IVF was Louise Joy Brown, born in England in 1978 and dubbed the first "test-tube" baby. IVF changed the scope of reproduction and offered new reproductive choices that created a new industry called "assisted reproductive technologies" (ART). IVF uses fertility-enhancing drugs that stimulate the ovary to develop multiple eggs during one hormonal cycle so more than just a single egg can be "harvested" (collected) during one procedure. Hormone treatment also stimulates the uterine lining, preparing it for **implantation** and pregnancy. Following a harvest, eggs are maintained under extremely sterile conditions, provided with nutrients and oxygen and allowed to mature. Then, sperm are added. Several days later, after fertilization can be confirmed, the dividing egg is placed into the woman's uterus through her **cervix**. If the embryo implants in the endometrium, pregnancy and fetal development are almost always normal.

This method of fertility enhancement is helpful if infertility stems from blocked or damaged oviducts (as was the case for Louise Brown's mother), or if female secretions prevent the sperm from accessing the egg. Excess eggs from a harvest can be frozen for use later, avoiding the trauma (and expense) of another harvest. Unfortunately, after almost 25 years, the success rate of IVF is only about 20%, requiring some couples to attempt this procedure several times. To increase the chances of IVF success, it is common

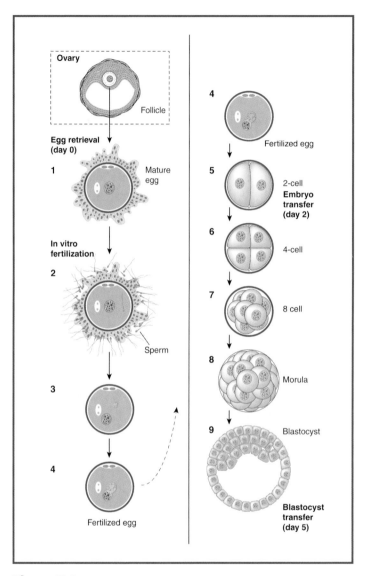

Figure 7.1 In vitro fertilization (IVF) or "fertilization in a test tube" (illustrated here) combines an ovum or ova with sperm outside the female reproductive system. Also at this time, hormones are given to the prospective mother, preparing the uterine lining for pregnancy. Once fertilization is confirmed, the zygote can be transferred to the mother's uterus at the 2-cell stage or later after the blastocyst stage has been achieved.

to transfer up to three embryos at once. Subsequently, multiple births are also common in IVF pregnancies when everything goes well.

Gamete intrafallopian transfer (GIFT) is a procedure that attempts to improve the success rate and simplify the IVF methodology. Eggs are again collected from a fertility-enhanced ovary. Then, in a procedure referred to as "band-aid surgery," GIFT places unfertilized eggs and sperm directly into an oviduct through a small incision in the woman's abdomen (which is then covered by a band-aid, hence the name). Although the GIFT procedure has a better success rate than IVF, GIFT still only claims a success rate of about 40%.

When all options have been exhausted, a couple may choose to hire another woman to be a surrogate mother.

ASSISTED REPRODUCTIVE TECHNOLOGIES (ART)

The discovery that a human could be conceived outside the human body caused somewhat of a stir in the beginning. There were groups that declared that man was "playing God" and the procedure was debated by ethicists, physicians, and religious leaders. As a result, the United States government banned the use of federal research money for ART research. The ban is still in force today, but the government stopped short of making *in vitro* fertilization illegal.

According to the Centers for Disease Control and Prevention, the 281 ART clinics in the United States make more than 59,000 attempts to produce a pregnancy each year. About 70% are *in vitro* fertilizations with transfer to the uterus through the cervix. The overall success rate for producing a live birth stands at 19.6% for all techniques and clinics combined. This calculates to 12,000 live births as a result of ART in just one year. As time passes, the success rate should increase.

The surrogate mother will become pregnant and bear a child for the couple. Depending on the status of the couple's infertility, the prospective parents may be able to contribute sperm, eggs, or both. Surrogate motherhood, however, can become tricky if conflicts over parenthood arise once the child is born.

CONTROLLING FERTILITY

There are many reasons people choose to control the timing of reproductive events. In this section, we will discuss methods of birth control that will allow an individual or couple to control fertility (Table 7.1). The purpose of any contraceptive method is to prevent pregnancy. To do this, a contraceptive device can either prevent sperm from reaching the egg by blocking the path, or by killing the sperm before it can reach the egg.

Abstinence is the only method of birth control that is 100% effective in the prevention of pregnancy. Abstinence is completely natural in that it does not rely on artificial methods of intervention such as condoms or chemical/hormonal contraceptives. This method has been shown to work for many people for short periods of time. For others, it is a lifelong decision.

Besides abstinence, some people prefer to rely on either the rhythm method (natural method) or the withdrawal method. The rhythm method relies upon the concept that fertilization is possible only for a limited time during the menstrual cycle, depending on the viability of the sperm or egg. To practice the natural method successfully, the couple must determine when ovulation occurs. The most popular method for determining time of ovulation is the temperature method. How does this work? A woman's body temperature rises slightly after ovulation. By taking her temperature every morning, a woman can pinpoint the day she ovulates. The rhythm method is much less effective than many of the other techniques because it requires a couple to avoid intercourse

(continued on page 82)

Birth Control Guide

Failure rates in this chart are based on information from clinical trials submitted to the Food and Drug Administration during product reviews. This number represents the percentage of women who become pregnant during the first year of use of a birth control method. For methods that the FDA does not review, such as periodic abstinence, numbers are estimated from published literature. For comparison, about 85 out of 100 sexually active women who wish to become pregnant would be expected to become pregnant in a year. The most effective way to avoid both pregnancy and sexually transmitted disease is to practice total abstinence (refrain from sexual contact).

This chart is a summary; it is not intended to be used alone. All product labeling should be followed carefully, and a health-care professional should be consulted for some methods.

Type of Contraceptive	FDA Approval Date	Description	Failure Rate (number of pregnancies expected per 100 women per year)	Some Risks (serious medical risks from contraceptives are rare)	Protection from Sexually Transmitted Diseases (STDs)	Convenience	Availability
Male Condom Latex/ Polyurethane	Latex: Use started before premarket approval was required. Polyurethane: cleared in 1989; available starting 1995.	A sheath placed over the erect penis blocking the passage of sperm.	11 (a, b)	Irritation and allergic reactions (less likely with polyurethane).	Except for abstinence, latex condoms are the best protection against STDs, including herpes and AIDS.	Applied immediately before intercourse; used only once and discarded. Polyurethane condoms are available for those with latex sensitivity.	Nonprescription
Female Condom	1993	A lubricated polyurethane sheath shaped similarly to the male condom. The closed end has a flexible ring that is inserted into the vagina.	21	Irritation and allergic reactions.	May give some STD protection; not as effective as latex condom.	Applied immediately before intercourse; used only once and discarded.	Nonprescription
Diaphragm with Spermicide	Use started before premarket approval was required.	A dome-shaped rubber disk with a flexible rim that covers the cervix so that sperm cannot reach the uterus. A spermicide is applied to the diaphragm before insertion.	17 (b, d, e)	Irritation and allergic reactions, urinary tract infection. (c) Risk of Toxic Shock Syndrome, a rare but serious infection, when kept in place longer than recommended.	None	Inserted before intercourse and left in place at least six hours after; can be left in place for 24 hours, with additional spermicide for repeated intercourse.	Prescription

Table 7.1

Type of Contraceptive	FDA Approval Date	Description	Failure Rate (number of pregnancies expected per 100 women per year)	Some Risks (serious medical risks from contraceptives are rare)	Protection from Sexually Transmitted Diseases (STDs)	Convenience	Availability
Cervical Cap with Spermicide	1988	A soft rubber cup with a round rim, which fits snugly around the cervix.	17 (b, d, e)	Irritation and allergic reactions, abnormal Pap test. (c) Risk of Toxic Shock Syndrome, a rare but serious infection, when kept in place longer than recommended.	None	May be difficult to insert; can remain in place for 48 hours without reapplying spermicide for repeated intercourse.	Prescription
Sponge with Spermicide	1983 (Not currently marketed).	A disk-shaped polyurethane device containing the spermicide nonoxynol-9.	14-28 (d, e)	Irritation and allergic reactions, difficulty in removal. (c) Risk of Toxic Shock Syndrome, a rare but serious infection, when kept in place longer than recommended.	None	Inserted before intercourse and protects for repeated acts of intercourse for 24 hours without additional spermicide; must be left in place for at least six hours after intercourse; must be removed within 30 hours of insertion. Is discarded after use.	Nonprescription; not currently marketed
Spermicide Alone	Use started before premarket approval was required. Starting November 2002, only one active ingredient is allowed.	A foam, cream, jelly, film, suppository, or tablet that contains nonoxynol-9, a sperm-killing chemical.	20-50 (studies have shown varying failure rates)	Irritation and allergic reactions, urinary tract infections (c).	None	Instructions vary; check labeling. Inserted between 5-90 minutes before intercourse and usually left in place at least 6-8 hours after.	Nonprescription

Table 7.1 *(continued)*

Type of Contraceptive	FDA Approval Date	Description	Failure Rate (number of pregnancies expected per 100 women per year)	Some Risks (serious medical risks from contraceptives are rare)	Protection from Sexually Transmitted Diseases (STDs)	Convenience	Availability
Oral Contraceptives—combined pill	First in 1960; most recent in 2000	A pill that suppresses ovulation by the combined actions of the hormones estrogen and progestin.	1	Dizziness; nausea; changes in menstruation, mood, and weight; rarely cardiovascular disease, including high blood pressure, blood clots, heart attack, and strokes.	None, except some protection against pelvic inflammatory disease.	Must be taken on daily schedule, regardless of frequency of intercourse.	Prescription
Oral Contraceptives—progestin-only minipill	1973	A pill containing only the hormone progestin that reduces and thickens cervical mucus to prevent the sperm from reaching the egg.	2	Irregular bleeding, weight gain, breast tenderness, less protection against ectopic pregnancy.	None	Must be taken on daily schedule, regardless of frequency of intercourse.	Prescription
Patch (Ortho Evra)	2001	Skin patch worn on the lower abdomen, buttocks, or upper body that releases the hormones progestin and estrogen into the bloodstream.	1 Appears to be less effective in women weighing more than 198 pounds.	Similar to oral contraceptives—combined pill.	None	New patch is applied once a week for 3 weeks. Patch is not worn during the fourth week, and woman has a menstrual period.	Prescription
Vaginal Contraceptive Ring (NuvaRing)	2001	A flexible ring about 2 inches in diameter that is inserted into the vagina and releases the hormones progestin and estrogen.	1	Vaginal discharge, vaginitis, irritation. Similar to oral contraceptives—combined pill.	None	Inserted by the woman; remains in the vagina for 3 weeks, then is removed for 1 week. If ring is expelled and remains out for more than 3 hours, another birth control method must be used until ring has been used continuously for 7 days.	Prescription

Type of Contraceptive	FDA Approval Date	Description	Failure Rate (number of pregnancies expected per 100 women per year)	Some Risks (serious medical risks from contraceptives are rare)	Protection from Sexually Transmitted Diseases (STDs)	Convenience	Availability
Post-Coital Contraceptives (Preven and Plan B)	1998-1999	Pills containing either progestin alone or progestin plus estrogen.	Almost 80 percent reduction in risk of pregnancy for a single act of unprotected sex.	Nausea, vomiting, abdominal pain, fatigue, headache.	None	Must be taken within 72 hours of having unprotected intercourse.	Prescription
Injection (Depo-Provera)	1992	An injectable progestin that inhibits ovulation, prevents sperm from reaching the egg, and prevents the fertilized egg from implanting in the uterus.	less than 1	Irregular bleeding, weight gain, breast tenderness, headaches.	None	One injection every three months.	Prescription
Injection (Lunelle)	2000	An injectable form of progestin and estrogen.	less than 1	Changes in menstrual cycle, weight gain. Similar to oral contraceptives— combined.	None	Injection given once a month.	Prescription
Implant (Norplant)	1990	Six matchstick-sized rubber rods that are surgically implanted under the skin of the upper arm, where they steadily release the contraceptive steroid levonorgestrel.	less than 1	Irregular bleeding, weight gain, breast tenderness, headaches, difficulty in removal.	None	Implanted by health-care provider in minor outpatient surgical procedure; effective for up to five years.	Prescription In July 2002, Norplant's manufacturer announced that it will no longer distribute the Norplant system. Women using the system should contact their doctors about what their contraceptive options will be after the five-year expiration date of their Norplant systems.

Table 7.1 *(continued)*

Type of Contraceptive	FDA Approval Date	Description	Failure Rate (number of pregnancies expected per 100 women per year)	Some Risks (serious medical risks from contraceptives are rare)	Protection from Sexually Transmitted Diseases (STDs)	Convenience	Availability
IUD (Intrauterine Device)	1976 (f)	A T-shaped device inserted into the uterus by a health professional.	less than 1	Cramps, bleeding, pelvic inflammatory disease, infertility, perforation of uterus.	None	After insertion by physician, can remain in place for up to 1–10 years, depending on type.	Prescription
Periodic Abstinence	N/A	To deliberately refrain from having sexual intercourse during times when pregnancy is more likely.	20	None	None	Requires frequent monitoring of body functions (for example, body temperature for one method).	Instructions from health-care provider
Surgical Sterilization— female	N/A	The woman's fallopian tubes are blocked so the egg and sperm can't meet in the fallopian tube, preventing conception. (g)	less than 1	Pain, bleeding, infection, other post surgical complications.	None	One-time surgical procedure.	Surgery
Surgical Sterilization— male	N/A	Sealing, tying, or cutting a man's vas deferens so that the sperm can't travel from the testicles to the penis. (g)	less than 1	Pain, bleeding, infection, other minor postsurgical complications.	None	One-time surgical procedure.	Surgery

(a) Projected from six-month study and adjusted for use of emergency contraception.
(b) If spermicides are used with barrier methods, be sure that the spermicide is compatible with the condom or diaphragm (won't cause it to weaken or break). Oil-based lubricants (such as petroleum jelly or baby oil) will cause latex to weaken and should not be used with these methods.
(c) Spermicides should not be used during pregnancy.
(d) Medications for vaginal yeast infections may decrease effectiveness of spermicides.
(e) Less effective for women who have had a baby because the birth process stretches the vagina and cervix, making it more difficult to achieve a proper fit.
(f) First approval date of currently marketed IUDs. Some IUDs were sold before premarket approval was required. Those products are no longer on the market.
(g) A contraceptive option for people who don't want children. Considered permanent because reversal is typically unsuccessful.

Source: Food and Drug Administration 8/02

(continued from page 76)

for an eight-day period in the middle of each menstrual cycle To be as effective as possible, couples practicing the rhythm method should abstain beginning five days before ovulation. This method would require that a woman's cycle be fairly consistent as it would be very difficult to determine where the middle of the month (ovulation) is if her cycle varies between 28 and 36 days. To be on the safe side, however, some doctors recommend that couples refrain from sexual intercourse from the first day of menstruation until four days after ovulation. In other words, this would mean no sex for 17 days of a 28 day cycle.

Even less effective is the withdrawal method or "coitus interruptus." Using this method, the man withdraws his penis from the vagina just before ejaculation. One major problem with this method is that sperm can be released before ejaculation occurs so there is a possibility of fertilization even if the man does not ejaculate.

Surgical sterilization can be a contraceptive option for both men and women. In males, the procedure is called a **vasectomy** (Figure 7.2) and can be performed in a doctor's office under local anesthesia. The doctor makes a small incision in the scrotum, locates each ductus deferens, ties them in two places and removes the section between the ties. This severs the pathway used to transport sperm to the outside of the body. With no access to the urethra, the sperm are reabsorbed by the testes. The benefit of a vasectomy is that the testes continue producing testosterone that maintains sexual interest and secondary sex characteristics, yet the man no longer can transport sperm into the vagina and therefore can not fertilize a woman's egg.

Sterilization in females is called a **tubal ligation** (Figure 7.3) and is a procedure very similar to a vasectomy. The doctor makes a small incision in the woman's abdominal wall, locates each oviduct, ties (ligates) each in two places, and cuts the tissue between the ties. This disrupts the pathway from ovary to uterus leaving no way for the oocyte to enter the uterus or

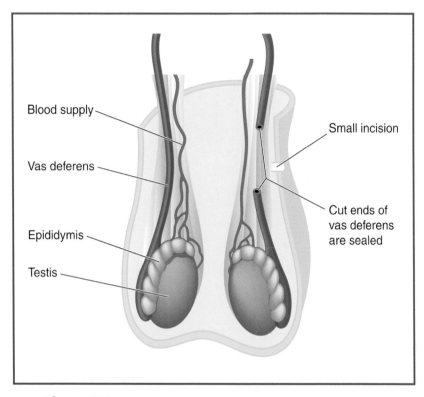

Figure 7.2 In males, surgical sterilization is accomplished by a minor procedure called a vasectomy (pictured here). The doctor makes a small incision in the scrotum and locates the vas deferens (ductus deferens). A small section of the vas deferens is removed and the cut ends are sealed either by ligation (tying the ends together) or by cauterization (heat). The procedure is then repeated on the other side. The sections that were removed are examined under a microscope to confirm that it was the vas deferens that was severed.

the sperm to reach the oocyte. Although it may be possible to reverse surgical sterilization, it is generally considered to be permanent. Therefore, committing to this type of birth control should be considered very carefully.

Manipulating the hormonally controlled menstrual cycle is another fairly effective method of birth control. The most common hormonal method is the oral contraceptive, or birth

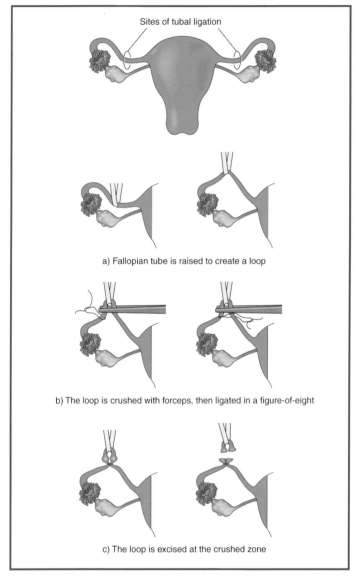

Sites of tubal ligation

a) Fallopian tube is raised to create a loop

b) The loop is crushed with forceps, then ligated in a figure-of-eight

c) The loop is excised at the crushed zone

Figure 7.3 Tubal ligation (illustrated here) in females is the equivalent of a vasectomy in males except a little more complicated since the doctor needs to enter the abdominal cavity to locate the fallopian tubes (oviducts). A portion of the fallopian tube is removed and the severed ends ligated (tied). This effectively blocks the pathway that delivers the egg to the uterus.

control pill. Birth control pills initiate and maintain a negative feedback loop by administering synthetic progesterone and estrogen in doses strong enough to inhibit the release of GnRH, LH, and FSH. In the absence of LH and FSH, follicles will not mature, and ovulation does not occur. However, if the pills are not taken daily, ovulation may resume and lead to an unexpected pregnancy.

National surveys estimate that more than 35% of women in the United States have used birth control pills at some time during their lives. Oral contraceptives have several side effects that can be considered both beneficial and harmful. For women who suffer from unusually severe menstrual cramps and abnormally heavy menstrual flow, oral contraceptives have been prescribed to reduce both cramps and menstrual flow. Other side effects include weight gain, headaches, high blood pressure, and blood clots. Women who smoke while on the pill have a higher risk of blood clots and vascular problems.

Other hormone-based contraceptives include timed release injection, dermal patch, and implants. In many countries outside the United States, slow acting injectable contraceptives are now being used. These injections are specially formulated progesterone and last up to three months. Implants placed under the skin are also a slow release form of progesterone formulated to protect an individual from pregnancy for up to five years, but they can be removed at any time if an individual's reproductive timetable changes. However, it is suggested that an individual not attempt conception until after the first normal hormonally controlled cycle. The newest method of hormonal contraception is the transdermal patch, a band-aid-like patch, impregnated with a cocktail of hormones including estrogen and progesterone. Each patch is worn for a week and then replaced. All of these methods have similar undesirable side effects to oral contraception including weight gain, headaches, and irregular menstrual cycles.

Intrauterine devices (IUDs) are small pieces of plastic or

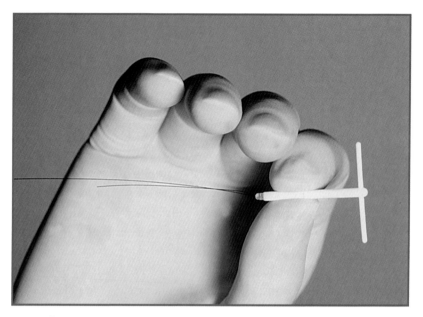

Figure 7.4 An intrauterine device (IUD) is one form of birth control. A small piece of plastic (although there are many different shapes and sizes), similar to the one pictured here, is placed into the uterus. The IUD creates a localized inflammation that causes an accumulation of white blood cells to the area. The resulting unfavorable environment prevents a fertilized egg from attaching to the uterine wall.

metal that are placed into the uterus by a physician or nurse (Figure 7.4). IUDs prevent pregnancy by creating a mild **chronic** inflammation within the uterine lining causing a slight increase in temperature and localized accumulation of white blood cells resulting in an environment that inhibits implantation of a fertilized egg. The benefit of this method is that it is relatively effective and the device can be removed at any time, but only by a qualified health-care provider. Some possible adverse effects to the presence of the IUD within the uterus include uterine cramping, infections, abnormal bleeding, and possible uterine damage.

Additional barrier devices include the diaphragm and

cervical cap for women and the condom for both men and women. Both the diaphragm and cervical cap must be fitted to the user's cervix by a physician. Both are fairly effective in preventing pregnancy, especially if they are used in conjunction with a **spermicide**. The major disadvantage to this method is that the device must be inserted just prior to intercourse and removed sometime after intercourse has ended. Over the past several decades, scientists have suggested that if a diaphragm is not inserted properly, it may actually enhance a woman's chances of getting pregnant by allowing sperm to pass to the uterine side where they are contained in close proximity to the cervix, enhancing the possibility that sperm would enter the uterus.

The condom is one of the most low-tech yet popular methods of contraception and is relatively effective if used properly. Both male and female condoms are available, although the male condom has been around longer and is much more popular. Under normal use, the condom is approximately 85% effective in preventing pregnancy. With perfect use (meaning couples make no mistakes in the way the condom is used and use a condom consistently) the percentage

INTERESTING FACTS

Condom use can be traced back several thousand years to the ancient Egyptians, who used a linen sheath to protect against disease. It was known that the condom was effective against disease, but it was not until the 1500s that this sheath was recognized as a method of preventing pregnancy. The first latex condom was made in 1880 but was not widely used until about 1930. By 1935, 1.5 million latex condoms were being produced each day in the United States. By 1993, the annual production of latex condoms worldwide had reached 8.5 billion.

http://www.avert.org/condoms.htm#2.

of effectiveness increases to 95% according to Advocates for Youth, which provides information on sexual health. If used in combination with a spermicide, condoms become even more effective in preventing pregnancy. The male condom is a thin latex or animal membrane that covers the penis and traps ejaculated sperm. The female condom is the newest condom on the market. This soft flexible liner fits into the vagina and collects sperm. It is highly recommended by doctors to protect women against AIDS and other sexually transmitted diseases. Of all the methods of contraception described, a latex condom (male or female but not animal membrane) is the only contraceptive method that also offers some protection against STDs, including AIDS.

When a woman believes her birth control method might have failed (a condom broke, she forgot to take her pill, or she had unprotected sex), a method commonly known as the "morning after pill" or "emergency contraception pill" is available. These pills deliver extremely high

WHICH TYPE OF CONDOM IS MOST EFFECTIVE AGAINST DISEASE?

If used correctly, latex condoms can help protect against disease. However, can the same be said for the natural membrane condoms? You can test this idea.

Mix clothing or food dye in a quart of warm water and fill latex and natural membrane condoms with equal volumes of the dye solution, seal them, rinse thoroughly, place each condom in a separate glass of water and observe for several hours.

Within an hour, you should notice some of the dye leaking through the natural membrane condom, but not the latex condom. Thus you can conclude that latex condoms are more effective than natural membrane condoms.

http://www.advocatesforyouth.org/publications/factsheet/fscondom.pdf

doses of progesterone and estrogen which help to prevent an unintentional pregnancy from occurring by stopping the ova from being released by the ovary. Many of these pills are effective if taken up to 72 hours after intercourse. A second morning after pill, RU-486, blocks the action of progesterone, making the endometrial lining of the uterus unsuitable to support an embryo. Developed in France, RU-486 became extremely controversial in the United States, where it became known, incorrectly, as the "abortion pill" because it is commonly prescribed after a pregnancy had been confirmed. Further, RU-486 has been shown to be effective in terminating a pregnancy for up to seven weeks after conception. In the United States, RU-486 was cleared for use by the FDA in the mid-1990s; however, political debate kept it from being available until the fall of 2000. Morning after pills are available by prescription only and should be used only under a doctor's supervision.

Unlike miscarriages, also referred to as spontaneous abortions, an elective **abortion** is an individual's choice to surgically terminate a pregnancy. Several methods of abortion include vacuum suction of the uterus, surgical scraping of the uterine lining, or infusion of a strong saline solution which results in the body rejecting the fetus. There are many physiological as well as psychological reasons for terminating a pregnancy, such as when continuing the pregnancy would endanger the mother's health, or in the case of rape or incest. Some women may choose to terminate the pregnancy if medical tests reveal severe birth defects or a **nonviable** fetus.

SEXUALLY TRANSMITTED DISEASES

Sexually transmitted diseases (STDs) can be spread by any form of sexual contact. This includes kissing, touching, anal, oral, and vaginal sex. Researchers suspect that the increase in STDs worldwide (Table 7.2) is the result of the

STD	Incidence (Estimated number of new cases every year)	Prevalence* (Estimated number of people currently infected)
Chlamydia	3 million	2 million
Gonorrhea	650,000	Not Available
Syphilis	70,000	Not Available
Herpes	1 million	45 million
Human Papillomavirus (hpv)	5.5 million	20 million
Hepatitis B	120,000	417,000
Trichomoniasis	5 million	Not Available
Bacterial Vaginosis**	Not Available	Not Available

*No recent surveys on national prevalence for gonorrhea, syphilis, trichomoniasis, or bacterial vaginosis have been conducted.

**Bacterial vaginosis is a genital infection that is not sexually transmitted but is associated with sexual intercourse.

Source: CATES, 1999

Table 7.2 The rates of STD incidences are on the rise. In 1999, over 85 million people were infected with an STD, according to the Centers for Disease Control and Prevention. Herpes is the most common STD, with over 45 million people infected worldwide.

declining age of first sexual contact and because contraceptive methods allow people to be sexually active without fear of pregnancy. About 25% of all cases of STDs each year are diagnosed in teenagers. Although transmitted by sexual contact, most STDs do not affect the organs of the reproductive system. STDs can be relatively hard to cure once a person has been infected. For some diseases, such as

AIDS, there are no known cures. Some STDs may result in extensive organ damage throughout the body, while a few may result in death.

STDs can be caused by bacteria, viruses, fungi, protozoa, and even arthropods (insects with jointed legs). Pubic lice are tiny arthropods related to spiders and crabs and are often referred to as "crabs." They live in hair, especially pubic hair, and are transmitted from one host to the next during sexual contact. They can also be transmitted by infected bed linen and clothes. Pubic lice receive nourishment by sucking blood from their host, causing intense itching and skin irritation. Pubic lice can be killed with antilice treatments.

Because most disease or parasitic organisms do not fair very well in the general environment, some preferred-entry sites are those that are warm and moist such as the respiratory system, digestive system, and the reproductive system during sexual intercourse. Some of the organisms that cause STDs, such as HIV, travel in body fluids. Others, such as pubic lice (crabs), take advantage of the opportunity afforded by intimate contact to transfer from one human to another.

Bacterial STDs include gonorrhea, syphilis, and chlamydia. Chlamydia is the most prevalent of all STDs, affecting 3–10 million people each year, many of them college students between the ages of 18–24 when sexual experimentation and numerous sexual partners are more common. Chlamydia is caused by a bacterium, and its symptoms in both men and women include a burning sensation during urination and mucus discharge. However, symptoms can be mild and may go undiagnosed, adding to the widespread infections among the college set. Women are diagnosed five times more often than men. This disparity is most likely due to the fact that women usually have regular checkups by their gynecologists. Public health officials suspect that many men go undiagnosed and that the actual number of people infected may be ten times higher than what is reported. If not treated, chlamydia may result in pelvic inflammatory disease, complications during pregnancy, and sterility. Children born to mothers with chlamydia can develop eye infections and pneumonia during birth by coming in contact with the infection as they pass through the birth canal.

Gonorrhea is extremely easy to contract. Approximately 50% of women and 20% of men become infected after only one exposure. As with chlamydia, during birth the child may become infected as it passes through the birth canal, developing a severe eye infection that could cause blindness. Symptoms of gonorrhea may disappear even if the infection remains. Because almost 20% of men and 80% of women infected with gonorrhea exhibit no symptoms, they are not aware that they need to seek medical attention and may pass the infection to others. If untreated, gonorrhea can cause inflammation and scarring of the oviducts, which may lead to sterility.

Syphilis, if left untreated, is potentially one of the most dangerous STDs. Syphilis exhibits three phases of development and infection that are separated by periods of time when the individual is **asymptomatic**. The initial phase can be identified 1–8 weeks after infection by the appearance of a hard dry sore called a **chancre** that contains bacteria. The chancre is a small painless sore that will usually develop in the genital region. It is easily visible when located on the penis but often goes unnoticed if occurring in the vagina or cervix. Generally, the sore will heal in about 1–5 weeks. About six weeks after the chancre heals, the infected individual will suffer a fever, headache, and loss of appetite, and lymph nodes in the neck, groin, and armpit enlarge as bacteria invade the body. This second phase lasts for 4–12 weeks after which the symptoms of Stage 2 syphilis may disappear for several years, and there is a possibility that the disease may not advance. However, individuals who progress to the third level are characterized by experiencing widespread damage to the nervous and cardiovascular systems leading to blindness, skin ulcers, **dementia**, and even death. The bacteria that cause syphilis can cross the blood-placenta barrier that normally protects the developing fetus from disease and toxins. A child developing in the uterus of an infected mother has a high probability of being born blind, malformed, suffering from neurological problems, or even stillborn (born dead).

All of these STDs can be treated with antibiotics. However, bacteria can and do develop a resistance to some antibiotics. This resistance has occurred in both gonorrhea and syphilis. Luckily, a new generation of broad spectrum antibiotics is effective in treating these STDs. However, overuse of these new antibiotics can result in another resistant strain of bacteria, rendering the new antibiotics ineffective.

Several decades ago, a person who had contracted gonorrhea or syphilis had to worry about the effectiveness of the current treatment. Today, if an individual goes to the doctor and finds out he (or she) *only* had gonorrhea or syphilis, he may be relieved that he does not have an incurable viral STD, such as human immunodeficiency virus (HIV), hepatitis B, genital herpes, or genital warts. HIV is one of the most dangerous STDs and is incurable. AIDS is the terminal phase of a disease caused by HIV infection. One of the most dangerous aspects of HIV/AIDS is its long asymptomatic stage that may last for 20 years or more while the carrier is infectious (but possibly does not know) and can transmit the infection to others.

Hepatitis B, transmitted by blood and body fluids, appears to be even more contagious than HIV. Hepatitis B causes inflammation of the liver, cirrhosis, and eventually complete liver failure. Each year, approximately 300,000 new cases are diagnosed. A vaccine for hepatitis B is available, and federal law mandates that all health care workers must be vaccinated. However, under normal circumstances, the average person would most likely never need to be vaccinated since the incidence of exposure to hepatitis B is extremely low.

More than 15% of the United States population is infected with genital herpes. Caused by the herpes simplex type 2 virus, symptoms include genital blisters, fever, and swollen **lymph nodes** in the groin. The symptoms occur sporadically and may disappear for long periods of time. There is no cure, only suppressive therapy. When the genital blisters are present, they can rupture and spread the virus, but during **remission**, the virus is not usually transmitted. There is no cure for herpes, but new drug treatments can suppress the active phase of the disease and make outbreaks rare. One of the dangers of herpes is a blister that forms undetected inside the woman's vagina. Since the blister is not visible, the woman would not be aware that she is contagious and would feel free to continue to have sex during this time, essentially passing the disease on to her partner. For that reason alone, it would be wise for an uninfected partner to be cautious and always use protection to prevent the spread of the virus.

CONNECTIONS

It is not all that uncommon for people to know someone who is having problems conceiving. However, while there are numerous individuals desperately attempting to get pregnant, there are many more individuals who seriously do not want to conceive a child. Each of these groups can benefit from research that has been conducted for more than 50 years. From the very simple to the more complex conditions that result in infertility, modern science has made great strides so that most individuals will be able to conceive. If the situation is such that an individual will never conceive or be able to carry to term, ethical considerations have made it possible to utilize a surrogate mother.

Recall that individuals wishing to have a certain degree

of control over their reproductive timing have any number of methods to choose that are safe and relatively effective. Therefore, modern science can offer help to those wishing to conceive a child as well as those who choose not to conceive.

Prior to the discovery of penicillin, sexually transmitted diseases were considered a terminal illness. However, with the discovery and development of modern antibiotics, some STDs no longer pose a serious threat provided the infected individual seeks medical attention. However, several relatively new STDs such as HIV/AIDS have been identified and are far more dangerous than gonorrhea or syphilis. These STDs are considered dangerous because they are, as yet, incurable and may remain that way for many decades to come.

Glossary

Abortion An elective procedure that terminates a pregnancy.

Abstinence Not having sexual intercourse.

Acrosomal reaction The release of enzymes and other proteins from the acrosome that occurs when a sperm has bound to the outer surface of the egg, helping the sperm to penetrate the outer layers of the egg.

Acrosome A cap-like structure covering the anterior two-thirds of the sperm head. It is a membrane-bound vesicle containing enzymes that digest a path to the ovum.

Adolescence The entire transition period between childhood and adulthood, not just sexual maturation.

Adrenal cortex The outer portion of an adrenal gland, divided into three zones: the zona glomerulosa secretes mainly aldosterone, the zona fasciculata secretes mainly cortisol, and the zona reticularis secretes mainly weak androgens.

Androgen A steroid hormone, producing or stimulating masculine characteristics, such as beard growth, lower voice, and larger muscles. This group of hormones contains the "male" sex steroid testosterone.

Asymptomatic Without symptoms.

Atresia Degeneration and reabsorption of an ovarian follicle before it fully matures and ruptures.

Autosome All chromosomes except the sex chromosomes (see *somatic*).

Basement membrane (basal lamina) A layer of nonliving material that anchors tissues to the underlying connective tissue.

Bipotential Cells or tissues that have the ability to develop into one of two distinct tissues. Usually the choice of which developmental path to take is controlled by internal or external stimuli.

Blood-testis barrier A functional barrier between the circulatory system and the cells of the testes, inhibiting the passage of certain substances from the blood into the seminiferous tubules.

Cervix The lower neck of the uterus that opens into the vagina.

Chancre A sore or lesion usually near or in the genital area.

Chromosome Rod-like structure of tightly coiled chromatin visible in the nucleus during cell division that carries all of the genetic information used by the body. In humans, there are 46 chromosomes, 44 somatic, and 2 sex chromosomes.

Chronic Constant and usually long lasting.

Clitoris An erectile organ of the female located at the anterior junction of the labia minora that is homologous to the male penis.

Clone A population of identical cells or organisms.

Collagen A protein that is the main organic constituent of connective tissue.

Collagenase An enzyme that denatures and digests collagen.

Corpus albicans The site of ovulation and the corpus luteum that has degenerated forming a white scar visible on the surface of the ovary.

Cytokinesis The division of the cytoplasm during cell division.

Defeminization The process of losing feminine characteristics, becoming more masculine.

Demasculinization The process of losing masculine characteristics, becoming more feminine.

Dementia A mental disorder characterized by the loss of memory, judgment, and abstract thinking. Often accompanied by changes in personality.

DNA (Deoxyribonucleic acid) A nucleic acid constructed of nucleotides consisting of one of four nitrogenous bases (adenine, cytosine, guanine, or thymine), deoxyribose, and a phosphate group; encoded in the nucleotides is genetic information of an organism.

Differentiation The process by which a cell alters its form and/or function.

Dihydrotestosterone (DHT) A hormone (converted from testosterone) responsible for differentiating the external genitalia into the penis and scrotum.

Diploid Having the number of chromosomes characteristically found in somatic cells of an organism. Symbolized 2*n*.

Egg An **ovum**; a mature female gamete. **Ova** (plural).

Ejaculation A forced discharge from the penis that contains seminal fluid and sperm.

Endometrium Inner lining of the uterus. The endometrium becomes thick and more vascular during the uterine cycle preparing for pregnancy.

Glossary

Enzyme A substance that affects the speed of chemical changes; an organic catalyst, usually a protein.

Epididymis A comma-shaped organ that lies along the posterior border of the testis and contains the ductus epididymis, in which sperm undergo maturation. Plural is **epididymides**.

Epithelial layer The tissue that forms glands, the superficial (outermost) part of the skin, lines blood vessels, hollow organs, and passages that lead externally from the body.

Fallopian tubes Duct that transports ova from the ovary to the uterus. Also called **uterine tube** or **oviduct**.

Feminization Acquiring female-like physiology and behaviors. When occurring in a male, these people are said to be demasculinized.

Follicle stimulating hormone (FSH) Hormone secreted by the anterior pituitary gland that initiates development of ova and stimulates the ovaries to secrete estrogens in females and initiates sperm production in males.

Fraternal Twins who come from two separate ova, fertilized by separate sperm; these individuals share no more characteristics in common than any other two siblings except for the same birth date.

Gamete Sex or germ cell containing a haploid number of chromosomes. Sperm and eggs are gametes.

Genetic profile The combination of chromosomes received from parents.

Genitalia External reproductive organs.

Genital ridge primordia Tissue found within the abdominal cavity that is destined to develop into the gonads.

Genital swellings In males, the genital swellings fuse to form the scrotum. In females the urethral folds and genital swellings develop into the labia minora and labia majora, respectively.

Genital tubercle A common primordia (primitive structure) at the indifferent stage. In males this structure enlarges forming the glans penis while in females it elongates forming the clitoris.

Germ cells A population of cells, set aside during development that generate all sex cells (spermatozoa and ova).

Glans penis The slightly enlarged region at the distal end of the penis.

Gonad A gland that produces gametes and hormones; the ovary in the female and the testis in the male.

Gonadotropin FSH and LH are collectively referred to as gonadotropins. They control secretion of the sex hormones by the gonads (ovaries and testes).

Gonadotropin releasing hormone (GnRH) Hypothalamic hormone that stimulates the gonadotropic hormone-secretory cells in the anterior pituitary, resulting in the secretion of LH and FSH.

Haploid Having half the number of chromosomes characteristically found in the somatic cells of an organism; characteristic of mature gametes. Symbolized *n*.

Hypothalamic-hypophyseal portal system An unusual capillary-to-capillary connection of the anatomical and functional link between the hypothalamus and anterior pituitary.

Hypothalamus Region of the brain forming the floor of the third ventricle. The hypothalamus helps regulate the body's internal environment by regulating the synthesis and release of the hormones of the pituitary gland.

Implantation The process where a fertilized ovum (or ova) becomes embedded into the endometrial lining of the uterus, developing a relationship to the maternal blood supply.

Inanimate A non-living object.

Indifferent phase A developmental stage in which a tissue or cell has not committed to a specific pathway or end-structure.

Infertile Not being capable of reproducing. Sterile.

Inflammatory reaction A non-specific defense response of the body to tissue injury characterized by the dilation of blood vessels resulting in redness, heat, swelling, and sometimes pain.

Innate Behaviors or drives that an individual is born with and does not need to experience or learn.

Interstitial cells of Leydig (interstitial endocrinocyte) Endocrine cells that synthesize and release testosterone; located in the connective tissue between seminiferous tubules in a mature testis.

Glossary

Labia majora Two longitudinal folds of skin extending downward and backward from the mons pubis of the female.

Labia minora Two small folds of mucous membrane lying medial to the labia majora of the female.

Lumen Cavity inside a tube, blood vessel, or hollow organ.

Luteinizing hormone (LH) Anterior pituitary hormone that aids maturation of cells in the ovary and initiates ovulation. In males, LH causes the Leydig cells of the testes to produce testosterone.

Lymph node A small mass of tissue and lymph vessels containing macrophages and lymphocytes that remove microorganisms, cellular debris, and abnormal cells from the lymph before it is returned to the circulatory system.

Masculinization Acquiring male-like physiology and behaviors. When occurring in a female, these people are said to be defeminized.

Meiosis Type of cell division that occurs during the production of gametes, involving two successive nuclear divisions resulting in daughter cells with a haploid (n) number of chromosomes.

Menarche The first menses (menstrual flow) and beginning of ovarian and uterine cycles.

Menstrual cycle (female reproductive cycle) General term for the ovarian and uterine cycles and the hormonal changes that accompany them. This also includes cyclic changes in the breasts, cervix, and the endometrium of a nonpregnant female that prepares the lining of the uterus to receive a fertilized ovum.

Migrate Organized and directed movement from one area to another.

Mitosis The division of the nucleus during cell division resulting in daughter cells containing the exact same complement of chromosomes.

Morphology The physical makeup of a tissue, organ, or organisim.

Müllerian ducts Primitive duct system present in all embryos. In females the Müllerian ducts differentiate into components of the reproductive tract. In males, Mullerian ducts degenerate under the influence of Mullerian Inhibiting Factor (MIF).

Müllerian inhibiting factor (MIF) A chemical secreted by the fetal testes that inhibits the development of the female reproductive tract so that ovaries, oviducts, and the uterus do not develop in the male.

Negative feedback The principle governing most physiological control systems. A mechanism of response in which a stimulus initiates actions that reverse or reduce the stimulus.

Nonviable Not able to sustain its own life.

Oocytes (oocyte, singular**)** Immature egg cell (ovum). A primary oocyte has not yet completed the first meiotic division; a secondary oocyte has begun the second meiotic division. A secondary oocyte, arrested at metaphase II, is ovulated.

Oogonia (oogonium, singular**)** The undifferentiated primordial germ cells in the fetal ovaries (comparable to the spermatogonia). No longer present at birth.

Ova Eggs in the female.

Ovary Female gonad that produces ova and the hormones estrogen and progesterone.

Ovulation The rupture of a mature ovarian follicle, releasing a secondary oocyte into the pelvic cavity.

Ovum The female reproductive or germ cell; an egg cell.

Perinatal The time period that encompasses events that occur shortly before birth until shortly after birth.

Physiological All processes carried out by the cells, tissues, organs, and organ systems to regulate and maintain a stable internal environment required for the proper functioning of the body.

Placenta The special structure through which the exchange of materials between fetal and maternal circulations occurs. Also called the afterbirth.

Polar body Small nonfunctional cell with almost no cytoplasm formed when the primary oocyte completes stage I of meiosis. Its primary function is to remove excess chromosomes.

Positive feedback A feedback mechanism in which the response enhances the original stimulus.

Glossary

Postnatal The period of time immediately after birth that lasts only a few days or weeks depending on the species.

Prenatal Events that occur prior to birth.

Prepubescent The period of time from the end of the postnatal period to puberty.

Primitive sex cords Early structures that form in the interior of the developing testes that will eventually form the seminiferous tubules in which all sperm will be produced throughout the life of a male.

Primordial Existing first; a primitive structure that will develop or mature into the functional tissues of an adult.

Prostaglandin A membrane-associated lipid; released in small quantities acting as a localized hormone.

Puberty The time of life during which the secondary sex characteristics begin to appear and the capability for sexual reproduction is possible; usually between the ages of 10–17.

Remission The situation where a disease regresses or disappears completely with treatment. Does not necessarily indicate the disease is cured.

Rete testis The segment of the sperm transporting duct system that connects the seminiferous tubules to the efferent ductules.

Semen The combined fluids from the seminal vesicles, prostate gland, and the bulbourethral glands that mix with and transport the sperm during an ejaculation.

Seminal vesicles A pair of convoluted, pouch-like structures, lying behind and below the urinary bladder and anterior of the rectum that secretes a component of semen into the ejaculatory ducts.

Seminiferous tubule A tightly coiled duct, located in the testis, where sperm are produced.

Sertoli cells Also called sustentacular or nurse cells. Nongerminal supporting cells in the seminiferous tubule. Sertoli cells are critical for the formation of the blood testes barrier, and support the developing sperm, and appear to participate in the transformation of spermatids into spermatozoa.

Sex chromosomes The twenty-third pair of chromosomes, designated X and Y, which determine the genetic sex of an individual; in males, the pair is XY; in females, XX.

Sexually dimorphic Structures and/or behaviors that differ between males and females.

Siblings Brother(s) and/or sister(s).

Somatic Having to do with the body. All of the cells of the body containing a diploid number of chromosomes. Does not include the sex cells (see **autosome**).

Spermatocyte Designated as primary or secondary, two stages of sperm development that occur from spermatogonium to mature sperm. Primary spermatocytes undergo the first meiotic division to produce the secondary spermatocytes.

Spermatogonia (spermatogonium, singular**)** Undifferentiated primordial germ cells located near the basement membrane of seminiferous tubules that generate all sperm produced by a male during his life (a type of stem cell).

Spermatozoa mature male gametes **(spermatozoon,** singular**).** Also referred to as **sperm** or **sperm cell**.

Spermicide Chemical specifically designed to kill sperm.

Stem cells Cells that remain relatively undifferentiated (unspecialized) and are able to divide and produce any number of different cells.

Steroid A lipid-based hormone derived from cholesterol that has three six-sided carbon rings and one five-sided carbon ring. These form the steroid hormones that are synthesized by the adrenal cortex and gonads.

Testosterone A male sex hormone (androgen) secreted by interstitial endocrinocytes (cells of Leydig) of a mature testis; needed for development of sperm; together with a second androgen, dihydrotestosterone (DHT), controls the growth and development of male reproductive organs, secondary sex characteristics, and body growth.

Thecal cells Cells making up the outermost layer of a developing follicle, surrounding the granulosa cells. Thecal cells are stimulated to synthesize and release androgens that are converted to estrogens in the granulosa cells.

Glossary

Tubal ligation A surgical method of sterilization in women that severs the oviduct, disrupting the pathway from the ovary to the uterus preventing sperm from reaching the egg or the egg reaching the uterus.

Tunica albuginea A dense white fibrous capsule covering of a testis and the tissue that penetrates deep to the surface of an ovary.

Unipotential A developing tissue that is programmed to develop in only one direction. If this tissue cannot develop as programmed, it will degenerate.

Urethral folds These folds fuse around the urethral groove to form the penis which encircles the urethra.

Vasa efferentia Portion of the sperm transporting duct system that connects the rete testes to the epididymis.

Vasectomy A minor surgical method of sterilization in men that severs the ductus deferens preventing sperm from exiting the body.

Vas deferens (ductus deferens) An accessory storage site for sperm and a section of the sperm transporting duct system that connects to the urethra.

Wolffian ducts In males, portions of the reproductive tract develops from the Wolffian ducts—a primitive duct system that develops in all embryos. In females, the Wolffian ducts degenerate.

GENERAL

Coustan, D.R. (ed) Haning, R.V., Jr. and Singer, D.B. (assoc. eds.). *Human Reproduction: Growth and Development.* Boston: Little, Brown and Co., 1995.

Jones, R.E. *Human Reproductive Biology.* 2nd ed. San Diego: Academic Press, 1997.

Sherwood, L. *Fundamentals of Physiology: A Human Perspective.* 2nd Ed. New York: West Publishing Co., 1994.

MALE REPRODUCTION

Burger, H., DeKrester, D. (eds). *The Testes.* New York: Raven Press, 1981.

Griffin, J.E. "The physiology of the testes and male reproductive tract and disorders of testicular function." In. Carr, B.R., Blackwell, R.E. (eds): *Textbook of Reproductive Medicine.* London: Prentice Hall, 1993. 221–245.

Veldhuis, J. "The hypothalamic-pituitary-testicular axis." In: Yen, S.S.C., Jaffe, R.B. (eds): *Reproductive Endocrinology.* 3rd ed. Philadelphia: WB Saunders. 1991, 409–459.

FEMALE REPRODUCTION

Chard, T., Grudzinskas, J.G. *The Uterus.* New York: Cambridge University Press, 1994.

Knobil, E. Neill, J.D. *The Physiology of Reproduction.* 2nd ed. New York: Raven Press, 1994. chaps. 4-7, 48-59.

SEXUAL DIMORPHISM

Arnold, A.P., Schlinger, B.A. "Sexual differentiation of brain and behavior: The zebra finch is not just a flying rat." *Brain, Behavior and Evolution.* 42 (1993): 231–241.

Collaer, M.L., Hines, M. "Human behavioral sex differences: A role for gonadal hormones during early development?" *Psychological Bulletin* 118 (1995): 55-107.

LeVay, S. "A difference in hypothalamic structure between heterosexual and homosexual men." *Science.* 253 (1991): 1034–1037.

Migeon, C.L., Wisiewski, A.B. "Sexual differentiation: From genes to gender." *Hormone Research.* 50 (1998): 245-251.

Bibliography

CONCERNS AND PROBLEMS

Fackelmann, K. "It's a Girl!" *Science News.* November 28, 1998.
Articles on how reproductive technologies can allow prospective parents to choose the sex of their child.

Gibbs, N. "The Pill Arrives." *Time.* October 9, 2000.
News story tracing the social debate in the U.S. over the use of the "morning after pill" RU-486.

Kaplan, L.J. and R. Tong. *Controlling Our Reproductive Destiny: A Technological and Philosophical Perspective.* Cambridge, Mass.: The MIT Press, 1994.
A look at birth control and fertility enhancement, including scientific, ethical, legal, and social indications.

Steptoe, P.C. and R.G. Edwards. 1978. "Birth after the reimplantation of a human embryo." *Lancet.* 2 (1978): 366.
Brief comment on the birth of the first test-tube baby.

GENERAL

www.merck.com/pubs/mmanual_home/contents.htm
The Merck Manual of Medical Information-Home Edition. Hormones: Male and Female Reproduction.

www.discoveryhealth.com
Discovery Health: His Health and Her Health sections. General Health Topics.

www.who.int/en
World Health Organization Home Page. Leads to a number of sections covering all aspects of human reproduction.

www.ucalgary.ca/UofC/eduweb/virtualembryo/initial.html
Dynamic Development: From Sperm and Egg to Embryo. This site is a Virtual Embryo learning resource.

INFERTILITY PROBLEMS

http://www.ihr.com/infertility/articles
Internet Health Reources: Infertility Resources. Photos and glossary of terms. See especially: *http://www.ihr.com/infertility/articles/infertility_photos.html*

http://www.nlm.nih.gov/medlineplus/infertility.html
National Library of Medicine and National Institutes of Health Web site on infertility.

STDS

http://www.ashastd.org/stdfaqs/index.html
American Social Health Association. Provides a glossary, with detailed information on each of the major STDs. Also condom information, statistics, and STD prevention.

http://www.advocatesforyouth.org
Advocates for Youth. Provides a wide range of sexuality topics, including STDs, HIV, and sexual orientation written specifically for adolescents.

Web Sites

HIV/AIDS

http://hivinsite.ucsf.edu
HIV InSite: University of California San Francisco knowledge base.

http://www.cdcnpin.org
Centers for Disease Control and Prevention National Prevention Information Network. Good resource for STD information. Also see additional CDC HIV info at *http://www.cdc.gov/hiv/dhap.htm.*

http://www.thebody.com/index.shtml
Another vast resource on HIV/AIDS. Emphasizes treatment—both on the symptom level on the side-effect level.

http://www.unaids.org
The United Nations Web site on HIV/AIDS.

Crooks, R., and K. Baur. *Our Sexuality*. 6th ed. Redwood City, Calif.: Benjamin/Cummings Publishing, 1996.
(An introduction to human sexuality)

Kaplan, L.J., and R. Tong. *Controlling Our Reproductive Destiny: A Technological and Philosophical Perspective*. Cambridge, Mass.: The MIT Press, 1994.
(Scientific, ethical, legal, and social implications of birth control and enhanced fertility.)

Steptoe, P.C., and R.G. Edwards. "Birth after the reimplantation of a human embryo." *Lancet* 2:366. (1978)
(Brief announcement of the birth of the first test-tube baby.)

Conversion Chart

Unit (metric)		Metric to English		English to Metric	
LENGTH					
Kilometer	km	1 km	0.62 mile (mi)	1 mile (mi)	1.609 km
Meter	m	1 m	3.28 feet (ft)	1 foot (ft)	0.305 m
Centimeter	cm	1 cm	0.394 inches (in)	1 inch (in)	2.54 cm
Millimeter	mm	1 mm	0.039 inches (in)	1 inch (in)	25.4 mm
Micrometer	µm				
WEIGHT (MASS)					
Kilogram	kg	1 kg	2.2 pounds (lbs)	1 pound (lbs)	0.454 kg
Gram	g	1 g	0.035 ounces (oz)	1 ounce (oz)	28.35 g
Milligram	mg				
Microgram	µg				
VOLUME					
Liter	L	1 L	1.06 quarts	1 gallon (gal)	3.785 L
				1 quart (qt)	0.94 L
				1 pint (pt)	0.47 L
Milliliter	mL or cc	1 mL	0.034 fluid ounce (fl oz)	1 fluid ounce (fl oz)	29.57 mL
Microliter	µL				
TEMPERATURE					
$°C = 5/9 \, (°F - 32)$		$°F = 9/5 \, (°C + 32)$			

Index

Index

Index

page:

12-13: Lambda Science Artwork

16-17: Lambda Science Artwork

18: Courtesy Randolph Krohmer

20: Lambda Science Artwork

23: © Noelle Nardone, based on design by Randolph Krohmer

26: Photo Lennart Nilsson/Albert Bonniers Forlag AB, A Child is Born, Dell Publishing Company

27: Lambda Science Artwork

30-32: Lambda Science Artwork

41: Courtesy Randolph Krohmer

45: Lambda Science Artwork

47: Lambda Science Artwork

51: © Donald Fawcett/Visuals Unlimited

53: © G. Shih and Richard Kessel/VU

60: Lambda Science Artwork

61: Lambda Science Artwork

66: Lambda Science Artwork

74: Lambda Science Artwork

77-81: Courtesy of the FDA

83: Lambda Science Artwork

84: Lambda Science Artwork

86: © SIU/Visuals Unlimited

90: *Tracking the Hidden Epidemics, Trends in STDs in the United States 2000*, Courtesy CDC

Viagra is a registered trademark of Pfizer Inc.

About the Author

Randolph W. Krohmer received a B.A. in 1974 from Coe College, Cedar Rapids, Iowa, with a major in biology and a certificate in secondary education. After teaching high school biology for three years, Dr. Krohmer entered the master's program at Saint Louis University, receiving an M.S. in biology in 1980. After a year as the Supervisor/Instructor of Histology at the SLU Medical School, he entered the Ph.D. program at SLU, receiving a Ph.D. in Biology in 1984. In the fall of 1984, Dr. Krohmer accepted a post-doctoral appointment at The University of Texas at Austin in the Institute of Reproductive Biology to conduct research in regulatory factors in vertebrate reproduction. In 1988, Dr. Krohmer accepted a post-doctoral appointment at Boston University in the Department of Biology to conduct research in the area of behavioral neuroendocrinology.

Dr. Krohmer began his tenure at Saint Xavier University in 1992 and served as Chair of the Department of Biology from 1995–98 and 2001–02. In 1993, he developed the Undergraduate Research Program in Biology which has enrolled more than 40 dedicated students who have learned various research techniques and participated in original research projects. Dr. Krohmer's research students have authored or coauthored 25 abstracts and three published manuscripts, and have presented numerous papers and talks at the regional, national, and international level.

Dr. Krohmer has received the Excellence in Scholarship Award in 1997, 2001, 2002, and 2003 and received the second annual Teacher/Scholar Award in 2001. Dr. Krohmer is the author of 20 scientific articles, more than 50 abstracts, and numerous lay articles for both children and adults.